D0470667

Activities for

Elementary School Social Studies

James W. Stockard, Jr.
Auburn University at Montgomery

WAVELAND
PRESS, INC.
Prospect Heights, Illinois

For information about this book, write or call:
    Waveland Press, Inc.
    P.O. Box 400
    Prospect Heights, IL 60070
    (847) 634-0081

7

This book
is dedicated to my family: wife Peggy
and children Renee, Jennifer, Trey, and Ashley,
and to my students and fellow faculty members in the
School of Education, Auburn University at Montgomery.

TABLE OF CONTENTS

CHAPTER 6: POLITICAL SCIENCE ACTIVITIES   **PAGE**

CHAPTER 7: INTERDISCIPLINARY ACTIVITIES   **PAGE**

Introduction
and Rationale

Pupil-participatory, activity-oriented, hands-on instruction has been advocated for the elementary school since shortly after the Civil War in America which ended in 1865. John Dewey (1859–1952) was one of the first Americans to champion an activity-oriented, learning-by-doing program for children in the elementary school. He was influenced by the ideas of European educators like John Amos Comenius (1592–1670), John Locke (1632–1704), Jean Jacques Rousseau (1712–1778), Johann Heinrich Pestalozzi (1746–1827), Johann Friedrich Herbart (1776–1841), and Friedrich Froebel (1782–1852) who all, in one way or another, had suggested that children learn best through experiences and activities; that children learn by doing.[1]

Real, hands-on materials, associated with a theme or topic of study, are the essence of developing interest, motivation, meaning, and true understanding in social studies classrooms. All higher-order thinking skills, according to Piaget, have their bases in activities involving concrete manipulation and observation.

The activities in this book are wide-ranging and can be adapted for many grade levels by increasing or decreasing the complexity of the activity. While the activities are categorized into the broad social science disciplines of geography, history, anthropology, sociology, economics, and political science, with one chapter devoted to interdisciplinary activities, all of the activities easily adapt to an integrative, interdisciplinary format.

Each activity follows the same easy-to-follow format, making the transition from one activity to another smoother and less troublesome. The key elements of each activity plan are:
- Topic (a descriptive title)
- Grade Level (usually adaptable for a span of grades)
- Activity Time (the time it normally takes to complete the activity)
- Materials Needed (a list of all materials needed to conduct the activity)
- Objectives (the resultant behaviors you want the children to exhibit)
- Introduction (starting the activity in an attention-getting way)
- Major Instructional Sequence (what you do, step-by-step)
- Closure or Evaluation (how you bring the activity to a conclusion)

By engaging your pupils in meaningful, worthwhile social studies activities, you are emphasizing the *processes* of learning rather than the *products*. The experience should be enriching to pupils and teacher alike!

---

[1] Adapted from Stockard, J., & Wolfinger, D. (in press). *Social studies for the elementary school child: An interdisciplinary approach.* Needham Heights, MA: Allyn & Bacon.

A Definition for Social Studies

Creating a suitable definition for social studies has been a difficult process for educators over time, but in 1993, the National Council for the Social Studies overwhelmingly adopted and approved the following definition. It has been embraced by educators in general and welcomed, accepted, and taken up by most teachers in the profession.

The NCSS definition of social studies...

Social studies is the integrated study of the social sciences and humanities to promote civic competence. Within the school program, social studies provides coordinated, systematic study drawing upon such disciplines as anthropology, archaeology, economics, geography, history, law, philosophy, political science, psychology, religion, and sociology, as well as appropriate content from the humanities, mathematics, and natural sciences. The primary purpose of social studies is to help young people develop the ability to make informed and reasoned decisions for the public good as citizens of a culturally diverse, democratic society in an interdependent world.[1]

---

[1] National Council for the Social Studies. (1994). *Curriculum standards for social studies: Expectations of excellence.* Washington, DC: National Council for the Social Studies (NCSS). Used by permission.

GEOGRAPHY

ACTIVITIES

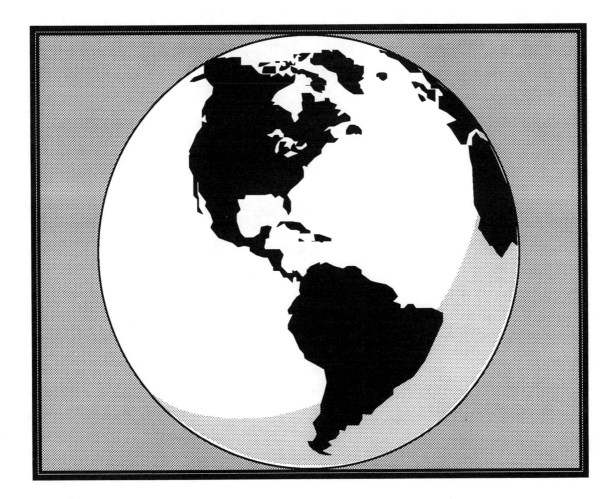

GEOGRAPHY ACTIVITIES

Introduction[1]

Geographers are interested in the location, variation, and interaction of human and physical elements on the Earth. They study where things are located on the Earth's surface and the reasons they are located there. The word geography was invented by the ancient Greek scholar, Eratosthenes. It is based on two Greek words: geo meaning "the Earth," and graphy, meaning "to write." The word geography, then, literally means to write about the Earth.

The geographer wants to answer two simple questions: where are people, places, and activities located on the Earth' surface and why are they located there? The geographer is interested in how people interact with their spatial environment. In a study of physical geography, the geographer is interested in landforms, water bodies, climate, weather, and plant and animal life. In studying cultural (human) geography, the geographer seeks information on how people interact with their physical and cultural environments. Human geography ranges from ways people live in selected cultures to other aspects of human settlement on Earth, such as historical, demographic, urban, economic, and political.

Traditionally, geography has occupied a key role in the social studies program of the elementary school. Too frequently, however, geography has been taught through memorizing facts and details, such as the names of state or national capitals, the population of an area, or the number of square miles in a state or country. Geography is a science that is concerned with the study and description of the Earth, and children can use the methods of the geographer to explore in and around the school site: careful observation of phenomena and recording data using simple charts. For example, they can carefully observe things in the neighborhood, like the number of deciduous and coniferous trees on the campus, and record the data on simple charts. They can make traverse maps of the areas surrounding the school that show such data as which houses are brick, which are wood; which houses have car shelters, which do not; which houses have trees, (deciduous, coniferous, both, or none); and the like. Early in their school experience, children should develop skill in using the tools of geography: charts, graphs, source-books, and especially, MAPS and GLOBES. Geographical insights and interest can often be achieved through posing hypothetical geographical propositions, such as, "What if Columbus had landed

---

[1] Adapted from Stockard, J. & Wolfinger, D. (in press). *Social studies for the elementary school child: An interdisciplinary approach.* Needham Heights, MA: Allyn & Bacon.

on the west coast of the United States?" Most educators agree that the elementary school is where geography must first be learned. Hopefully, geography will be taught in a way that will help the population become geographically literate. Hopefully, elementary school geography will lead to mastery, assuring literacy in geography, and motivating people to continue geographic growth through lifetime learning.

The Five Fundamental Themes of Geography

In the early 1980s, the National Council for Geographic Education (NCGE) and the Association of American Geographers (AAG) worked jointly to produce guidelines for studying geography in elementary and secondary schools. The guidelines, which were published in 1984, embodied five fundamental themes for teaching geography which have been widely used by curriculum planners to infuse more geography teaching into the social studies. Later, in 1985, the National Geographic Society (NGS) and the American Geographical Society (AGS) joined with the NCGE and the AAG to form the Geographic Education National Implementation Project, known widely by its acronym, GENIP. Under GENIP, each organization works to improve the quality of geographic education and to promote the five fundamental themes of geography. Much has been accomplished by GENIP, such as Congress establishing a National Geography Awareness Week, and by its individual members. For example, the NGS sponsors summer geography institutes for teachers through a Geographic Alliance which has spread its roots to every state and into hundreds of county and local school systems across America. The Geographic Alliance has deepened and broadened the geographic interest and knowledge of literally thousands of teachers and is having a profound effect on improving geographic education. The five fundamental themes are location, place, relationships within places, movement, and regions, and are described as follows:

Location is position on the earth's surface. Absolute location (the earth's geographic graticule or grid system, i.e., latitude and longitude) and relative location (Monroe is 100 miles east of Shreveport; Destin is 45 miles west of Panama City) are used to describe positions of people and places on the earth's surface.

Place is characterized by physical and human characteristics. Physical characteristics include landforms, bodies of water, climate, soils, animal life, and natural vegetation. Human characteristics include languages, religions, settlement patterns, systems of transportation, vocational attributes, and the like. Together, these characteristics distinguish one place from another.

Relationships within places considers the advantages and disadvantages of human settlement on the earth; and the ways in which people modify and adapt to the environment of a place. Often, for example, we find dense population settlements along flood plains where the soil is fertile for crop growth, river transportation is available, and water resources are abundant. Occasionally, however, the river runs rampant and floods the population settlements, often with disastrous results. In contrast, low densities of population are usually found in deserts where there are more disadvantages for human settlement. The technological capabilities of humankind, however, often allow places to be modified where settlement can occur in desert areas (Israel, for example), and where fewer catastrophes befall those living on flood plains (dams, revetments to river embankments, and the like).

Movement pertains to how humans interact with each other on the earth via the movement of people, ideas, goods, and services.. People travel from one place to another, communicate with each other, and depend upon one another for products, information, ideas, and the like, which might not exist in their immediate environments.

Regions refer to areas that display unity in terms of selected criteria, such as type of government, type of landform, language group, environmental features, religion, and the like. Geographers are interested in studying how regions form and how they change.

Topic: COMPARING MODELED, MAPPED, AND REAL OBJECTS

Grade Level: K-2   **Activity Time:** 1 class period

Materials Needed:
1. models of cars, trains, planes, houses, and the like
2. pictures of cars, trains, planes, houses, and the like
3. picture maps showing neighborhoods, houses, businesses, streets, and the like

Objectives:
As a result of this activity, the learner will:
- distinguish between models and the real thing.
- distinguish between pictures and the real thing.
- distinguish between mapped representations and the real thing.

Introduction:
1. Place the models, pictures, and picture maps on a large table and invite the children to explore the objects on the table.
2. Let children hold the objects, play with them, and examine them closely.

Major Instructional Sequence:
1. Have pupils gather around the table in a large, loose circle.
2. Hold up one of the models, the car for example, and ask, "How is this like a real car?" Pupils will generally relate that it looks like a real car, is shaped like a real car, has wheels like a real car, and the like. Ask, "How is this different from a real car?" Pupils will generally relate that it is much smaller, doesn't really work (like a car), is too small for people to get into, and the like. Elaborate on the fact that it is a *model* of a real car.
3. Hold up one of the pictures and go through the same procedure, but relating to the picture and the object, thing, or person it represents.
4. Call attention to pictures and symbols on the map and go through the same procedure, but relating to the map and what it represents.

Closure or Evaluation

1. Have each pupil select an object from the table, either a model, a picture, or a map.
2. Take turns letting each pupil explain what he/she is holding and how it relates to the real thing.
3. Once everyone has had a turn, have each pupil select another object, but different from the one they had before. For example, if a child selected a model for the first turn, then either a map or picture must be selected for the second turn.
4. Continue in this fashion until each pupil has had a model, a picture, and a map.

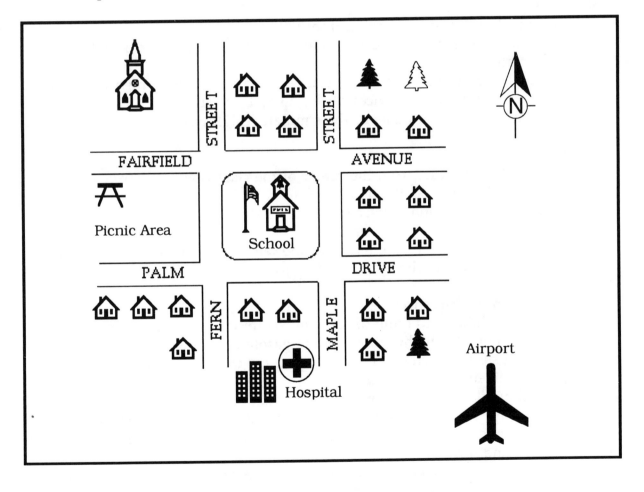

Topic: CONSTRUCTING A HIGHWAY COMMUNITY

Grade Level: K-2   **Activity Time:** 2 days

Materials Needed:
1. long strip of butcher paper (15 to 20 feet long)
2. empty milk cartons, cereal boxes, etc. (to represent buildings)
3. toy car
4. marking pens
5. tempera paints and brushes

Objectives:
As a result of this activity, the learner will:
- construct a highway community using the butcher paper and the cartons.
- think of needs people might have when traveling along a highway.
- create simulated services for highway travelers.
- develop mental maps of the simulated highway community.

Introduction:
1. Move the furniture from the center of the classroom and stretch the butcher paper down the middle of the floor.
2. Have pupils sit along each side of the paper strip. Tell them the strip is a highway connecting two distant towns.
3. Drive a toy car along the highway and tell pupils it takes hours to drive from one town to the other.

Major Instructional Sequence:
1. Ask the children to think of some of the things that might happen as one drives along the highway. (Needing gasoline, getting hungry, getting tired, getting sleepy, having a flat tire, having car trouble, etc., are some of the things likely to be mentioned.)
2. Lead pupils in a discussion of services that might be needed along the highway. (They will likely mention a gas station, garage, fast-food restaurant, an expensive restaurant, motel, a convenience grocery store, a bank, and the like.)
3. As services and facilities are mentioned, ask for someone who will operate the gas station, the restaurant, etc., and give that person a carton to place along the highway.
4. Help pupils decide the best locations for their businesses.
5. As the highway community grows, other needs will surface: churches,

homes, a power company, a bank. Let pupils use the cartons to represent these new services and businesses and place them appropriately in the highway community.

6. Lead pupils in a discussion to decide on a community name and to think about problems which might occur, such as the need for law enforcement for speeders and crime, for example.

Closure or Evaluation

1. Work in cooperative groups to draw large maps of the highway community on butcher paper, construction paper, or the like, using marking pens and tempera paints.
2. Hang the maps as exhibits around the room.

Topic: UNDERSTANDING GLOBES AS MODELS OF THE EARTH

Grade Level: 1–3   **Activity Time:** 1 class period

Materials Needed:
1.   toy car
2.   globe (several globes if possible)
3.   drawing paper, pencils, and crayons

Objectives:
   As a result of this activity, the learner will:
   • identify the globe as the model of the Earth.
   • describe the globe as a sphere (ball shape).
   • identify land and water on the globe.
   • draw a globe.

Introduction:
1.   Hold up toy car; pass around for examination.
2.   Ask pupils to identify car windows, doors, wheels, and the like.
3.   Have pupils associate small car to real car. Elicit responses that toy car is smaller than real car.
4.   Explain that toy car is model of real car.

Major Instructional Sequence:
1.   Hold up globe; pass around for examination.
2.   Explain that the globe is a model of the Earth. The Earth is much larger than the globe, but it is the same shape (ball/sphere).
3.   Discuss land and water forms on the globe. The blue part is water and the colored part is land.
4.   Have pupils point to parts of the globe and identify as land or water.

Closure or Evaluation
1.   Let pupils draw globes and color them.

Topic: UNDERSTANDING MAPS AS PICTURES OF THE EARTH

Grade Level: 1–3   **Activity Time:** 1 class period

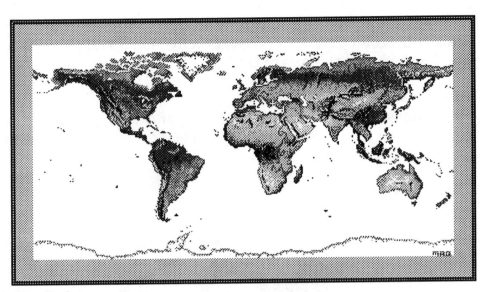

Materials Needed:
1. globe
2. map
3. child's picture
4. large book (preferably a children's atlas)

Objectives:
As a result of this activity, the learner will:
- identify a map as a picture of the Earth.
- locate land and water on globe and map.

Introduction:
1. Show globe and review the previous activity, Understanding Globes as Models of the Earth. Have pupils use globe to explain that the Earth is a (ball) sphere and has land and water on it.

Major Instructional Sequence:
1. Show a map and explain that the map is a picture of our world. Explain that the map is flat, but our world is not flat; just as a picture of a child is flat, but the child is not flat. Show picture of child and compare.
2. Explain the need for maps by trying to put a globe in a book. Ask pupils what happens when you try to fit a globe into a book (the book won't close). Explain that people wanted to put the globe in a book but since it

wouldn't fit, they had to cut the globe and pull it apart to make a flat map or a picture of our Earth.

3.   Explain to pupils that the water on the map is still blue and the land is still a different color or colors.

Note – this is a good time to explain to children that the land is not actually the color/colors that appear on the map. Walk outside, if possible, and look at colors of landscape.

Closure or Evaluation

1.   Have pupils take turns tossing a bean bag or dropping an object such as a cube onto the map. Next, have pupils identify the place where the object landed as land or water.

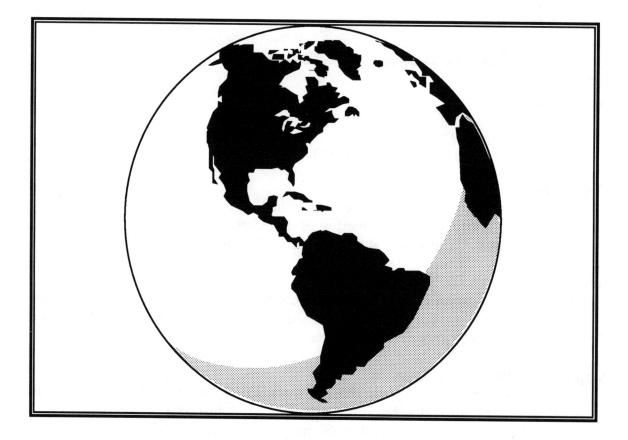

Topic: MAKING A SANDBOX PLAYGROUND

Grade Level: K-3   **Activity Time:** 1 class period

Materials Needed:
1. large sandbox (either in the classroom or outside)
2. bowls of green colored sand or rice (use food coloring to make)
3. popsicle sticks, pipe cleaners (felt-covered wire)

Objectives:
As a result of this activity, the learner will:
- construct replicas of real and imagined areas.
- use symbols to represent real objects.
- understand that symbols represent real objects.
- understand that a model playground can represent a real playground.

Introduction:
1. Take pupils on a walking tour of the school playground.
2. Stop to note grassy areas, ball fields, playground equipment, fences, and the like.
3. Call attention to whether the area is sloping, hilly, or flat.

Major Instructional Sequence:
1. Gather pupils around the sandbox. Tell them they are going to make a map of the playground in the sandbox.
2. Assist children in shaping the sand to model the slopes, hills, or flatness of the playground.
3. Use the colored sand (or rice) to represent grassy areas.
4. Use the popsicle sticks and pipe cleaners to make models of the playground equipment, fences, and children playing.

Closure or Evaluation
1. Let children take turns describing the components of the sandbox playground in a round-robin discussion, explaining the parts they participated in making. Invite parents and pupils from other classrooms to come by and view the sandbox playground. Have pupils take responsibility for telling visitors about the sandbox playground.
3. In the future, use the sandbox to create maps of imagined areas in well-known children's stories, such as "Little Red Riding Hood" and "The Three Little Pigs."

Topic: NORTH AMERICA AND OTHER CONTINENTS

Grade Level: 1–3   **Activity Time:** 1 class period

Materials Needed:
1.   globe
2.   continent map
3.   North America cut-out-pieces (one for demo, one for each pupil)
4.   atlas
5.   child's map* (blue construction or bulletin-board paper 24" X 17" with outlines of continents pre-drawn by teacher
6.   crayons, glue

Objectives:
As a result of this activity, the learner will:
*   identify the number of continents on the map.
*   describe North America as the continent on which we live.

Introduction:
1.   Review globe and have pupils describe it as a model of the Earth.
2.   Describe the land areas as continents.
3.   Count, point to, and name the continents on the globe.

Major Instructional Sequence:
1. Show continent map; describe the land as continents.
2. Count the continents; let different pupils help by touching continents as they count them. (Pronounce names of continents as they are touched; let pupils say names with you.)
3. Put your North America cut-out-piece on the map and identify it as the continent on which we live.
4. Find North America on the globe.
5. Locate North America in the atlas.
6. Have each child point to continent outlines on their maps.*

Closure or Evaluation
1. Each child colors in a cut-out piece of North America and glues it to his/her map.*

Topic: DISCOVERING CARDINAL DIRECTIONS

Grade Level: 2-3   **Activity Time:**   1 class period

Materials Needed:
1.   felt-tip marking pens
2.   cardboard squares, about 12" X 12" (four needed)

Objectives:
    As a result of this activity, the learner will:
- determine which direction is North.
- determine the other cardinal directions (West, East, South).
- label the walls of the classroom with the cardinal directions.

Introduction:
1.   Show pupils a globe.
2.   Identify the North Pole and the South Pole.
3.   Tell children that they are going outside to discover the direction of the

North Pole.

Major Instructional Sequence:
1. On a sunny day in winter, about noon, take class outside.
2. Have pupils stand so that their shadows are directly in front of them.
3. Tell them that when they find their shadows directly in front of them, they are facing North (toward the North Pole).
4. Have pupils stretch out their arms; their left arms point West, their right arms point East, and South is directly behind them (toward the South Pole).
5. Back inside the classroom, have pupils cooperate to label the pieces of cardboard "North," "South," "East," and "West."
6. Tape the cards on the classroom walls to indicate the four cardinal directions, North, South, East, and West.

Closure or Evaluation
1. Frequently identify areas of the room based on the cardinal directions, such as "the table to the South," "the learning center on the East wall," "the group on the West side," and the like.

Topic: TRAVELING ON LAND AND WATER

Grade Level: 1–3   **Activity Time:** 1 class period

Materials Needed:
1.   globe
2.   map
3.   water table with water, blue food coloring, sand (water table has water with blue food coloring surrounded by sand to represent land areas)
4.   bowls
5.   toy boats, cars, and airplanes; toy person
6.   drawing paper, pencils, and crayons

Objectives:
  As a result of this activity, the learner will:
  • locate land and water.
  • identify vehicles that travel on land and water.
  • describe and defend how he/she would travel from one body of land to another.

Introduction:
1.   Introduce globe and map; review land and water forms on both.

2.   Ask children to describe a map; explain what it is (picture of the Earth).

Major Instructional Sequence:
1.   Introduce water table.
2.   Have pupils point to land and water.
3.   Show vehicles — boats, cars, airplanes; have children explain how each vehicle travels.
4.   Demonstrate movement of vehicles on water table.
5.   Pass out vehicles and have each pupil demonstrate how his/her vehicle travels. Ask why boats cannot travel on land and why cars cannot travel on water.
6.   Put model of a child/person on piece of land. Point to another piece of land and ask how the person can get there. Have pupils model the movement and explain.
7.   Put model of a child or person on a piece of land and point to another spot on the same piece of land — ask how person can get from that spot to the other.
8.   Repeat same movement exercises on globe and on map.

Closure or Evaluation
1.   Have pupils draw map with land and water including a vehicle or vehicles for traveling from one area to another.

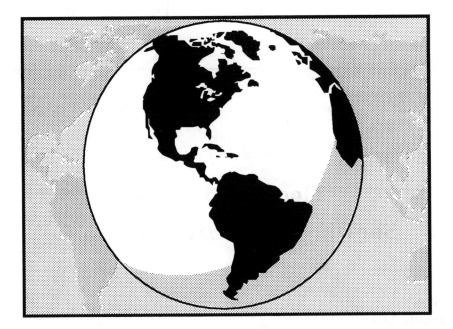

Topic: A FLOOR GRID SYSTEM

Grade Level: 1-3   **Activity Time:** 1 class period

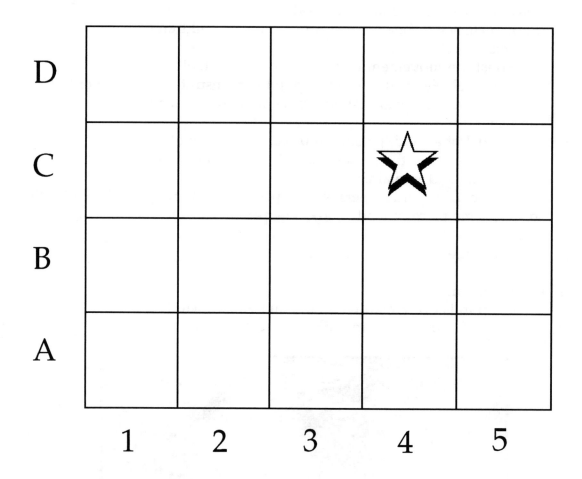

Floor Grid System
Showing Cardboard Star in C-4

Materials Needed:
1. masking tape
2. cut-out of a cardboard star (about 6 to 8 inches in diameter)

Objectives:
> As a result of this activity, the learner will:
> - find coordinates in a grid system.
> - locate objects in a grid based on their coordinates.

Introduction:
> 1. Have children assist in using the masking tape to make a grid system on the floor similar to the illustration above.
> 2. Place the cardboard star in a grid and give its coordinates. For example, "The star is in C-4. Why do I say that is where the star is?" Encourage discussion. Help pupils to understand why you said the star was in C-4.

Major Instructional Sequence:
> 1. Place the star in a grid space.
> 2. Ask, "Raise your hand if you can tell me where the star is."
> 3. Let the person who correctly identifies the location of the star retrieve it, move it to a new grid location, and ask for someone to identify the new location.
> 4. Continue in this manner until all children have successfully located the star one or more times.

Closure or Evaluation
> 1. As a variation, put various pieces of fruit in the grid and let the pupils who identify the coordinates retrieve (and eat) the fruit.
> 2. Have children stand in grid squares when they are given the coordinates for direction.

Topic: NORTH AMERICA AND SOUTH AMERICA

Grade Level: 1–3   **Activity Time:** 1 class period

Materials Needed:
1. globe
2. continent map
3. North America and South America cut-out-pieces (one for demo, one for each pupil)
4. atlas
5. child's map* (blue construction or bulletin-board paper 24" X 17" with outlines of continents pre-drawn by teacher)
6. crayons, glue

Objectives:
As a result of this activity, the learner will:
- identify North America as the continent on which we live.
- identify South America as the continent below (south of) North America.

Introduction:
1. Show globe and review concepts from previously taught activities. Example: (a) a globe is a model of the Earth; (b) a map is picture of the

Earth; (c) we call the land on maps continents; (d) there are seven continents.

Major Instructional Sequence:
1. Ask pupils to locate North America on globe and map. Match your demo piece with North America on the map. Ask what they know about North America.
2. Locate North America in the atlas and have pupils name it.
3. Show map and hold up your demo piece of South America.
4. Pupils find South America on the map and match the demo piece with South America on the map.
5. Pupils find South America on the globe.
6. Show South America in the atlas and discuss.

Closure or Evaluation
1. Each child colors in cut-out pieces of North and South America and glues them to his/her map.*

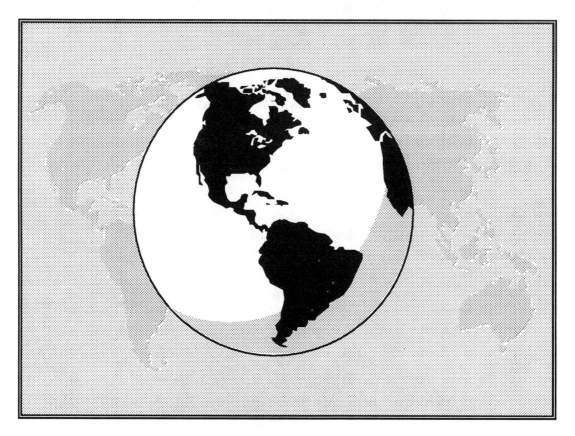

Topic: UNDERSTANDING RELATIVE LOCATION

Grade Level: K-3   **Activity Time:** 1 class period

Materials Needed:
1. transparency map of the classroom (prepared by teacher)
3. large, unlined index cards (5" X 7")
4. black marking pen
5. Scotch tape
6. pencils, notebook paper

Objectives:
As a result of this activity, the learner will:
- orient to different positions in the classroom.
- find objects and items based on relative location.
- play the "Simon Says" game with relative location directions.
- list objects based on their relative location on a classroom map.

Introduction:
1. Have each pupil carefully print his/her name on the index card with the marking pen (teacher prints names for younger children).
2. Tape the identification cards to the top of each pupil's chair.
3. Line pupils along the wall and play a quick game of "Simon Says," using

commands that orient toward a different position. For example, "Simon says go to the front wall, to the back wall, behind Jimmy's chair, in front of Pam's chair, near the pencil sharpener, under the map." Continue until a winner is evident or after enough time has elapsed to assure that all have grasped the idea of relative location.

Major Instructional Sequence:
1. With pupils lined along the wall, practice relative location with individual pupils giving and receiving up to three-step relative location directions. For example, Pam says, "Who can stand behind Jimmy's chair, in front of Ellen's chair, and then beside the large bulletin board?" Pam selects a volunteer. If the person selected accomplishes the three-step relative location directions successfully, they give the next directions. Continue in this fashion until all pupils have had at least one opportunity to be successful.

Closure or Evaluation
1. Place the transparency map of the classroom on the overhead.
2. Ask pupils to record their answers to the following questions on a sheet of notebook paper. (For younger pupils, solicit oral responses.) Ask various relative location questions, such as, "Which chair is three places in front of Don's chair?" Let each pupil check his/her own paper as you point out the answers on the overhead transparency map.

Topic: LOCATING MEXICO AND CANADA: UNDERSTANDING
THE CLIMATIC DIFFERENCES

Grade Level: 2-4   **Activity Time:** 1 class period

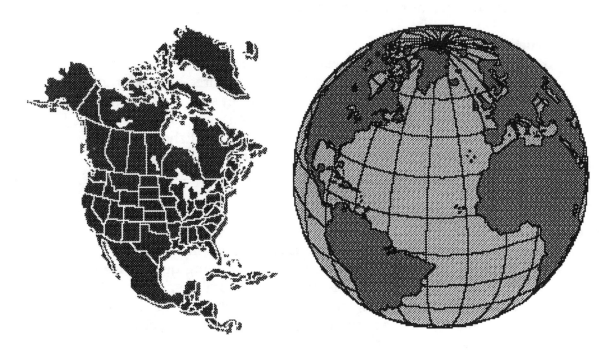

Materials Needed:
1.   globe
2.   world map or Western Hemisphere map or North American map
3.   catalogs, newspapers, magazines, etc. containing pictures of clothes
4.   paper, pencils, scissors, paste

Objectives:
As a result of this activity, the learner will:
- point to Canada and Mexico on a map and globe.
- show that Canada is north of the United States.
- show that Mexico is south of the United States.
- tell why climates are different in Mexico and Canada.

Introduction:
1.   Show the United States on a globe and world map and have pupils locate the neighbors to the north and south.
2.   Ask if anyone knows the names of these neighboring countries. Identify the countries as Canada (to the North) and Mexico (to the South). Have

pupils point to these countries on the globe and map and say "Canada" or "Mexico." Ask if anyone has ever been to one of these countries or if they know of anyone who has been. If so, let pupils tell about it and have appropriate discussion.

Major Instructional Sequence:
1. Point out the equator on the globe and on the map.
2. Let pupils touch the equator on the globe and map.
3. Remind pupils that the further north (or south) you travel from the equator, the colder the climate, and the closer you move to the equator, the warmer the climate.
4. Let pupils examine the globe and map and decide which country is warmer (Mexico) and which country is colder (Canada).
5. Lead pupils in a discussion on how clothing in Canada might differ from clothing in Mexico.

Closure or Evaluation
1. Each child makes a two-column shopping list: (a) Clothes for Canada, and (b) Clothes for Mexico. Provide pictures from catalogs or ads from newspapers and magazines for pupils to cut out and paste in the appropriate column.

Topic: STATE IDENTIFICATION

Grade Level: 3-6   **Activity Time:** 2 days

Materials Needed:
1. globe, large U. S. political wall map
2. construction paper
3. marking pens, scissors
4. large cardboard box

Objectives:
As a result of this activity, the learner will:
- reproduce state shapes from a U. S. map.
- identify each state shape with the name of the state.
- find and list factual information on a specific state.

Introduction:
1. Using the large U. S. political wall map, talk about:
   - small states.
   - large states.
   - coastal states.
   - interior states.
   - states with unusual shapes.
2. Have various pupils come up and point to some of the states identified.

3.   Tell pupils they are going to create and play a game with state shapes.

Major Instructional Sequence:
1.   Divide pupils into five cooperative work groups. Each group will be responsible for ten states (assigned by teacher).
2.   The groups make an outline of their states, cut them out, color and decorate them with state landmarks (cities, rivers, lakes, and the like, from material provided by the teacher) and write the name of the state on the back.
3.   All state cut-outs are placed in the large cardboard box.
4.   Select a pupil to go to the box, draw a state, hold it toward the class so the name won't show, and ask for hands of those who can identify the state.
5.   When a correct identification is made, the pupil making the correct identification draws the next state. (No one can participate more than once until everyone has had at least one turn.)

Closure or Evaluation
1.   One at a time, blindfold pupils and let them reach into the box of state cut-outs and select a state.
2.   Pupils research specific facts on the state they get from the box, such as population size, land area, location, motto, state flower, state bird, major cities, neighboring states, major universities, and the like.
3.   Each pupil holds up his/her state cut-out, shows where it is located on the wall map of the United States, and gives the factual data gathered.

Topic: SOAP-DOUGH REGIONAL MAPS

Grade Level: 3-6   **Activity Time:**   2 days

Materials Needed:
1.   detergent powder (Ivory Snow, Cheer, Tide)
2.   water
3.   food coloring
4.   cardboard and scissors
5.   plastic bowls
6.   map of United States

Objectives:
    As a result of this activity, the learner will:
   - produce a regional map of soap-dough.
   - use different colors to represent different regions.
   - place regions together to form a regional map of the United States.
   - label the regions of the United States.

Introduction:
1.   Using a map of the United States, have volunteers point to the state where they live.
2.   Explain and demonstrate how the state is a part of a region. Identify the states in the home region.
3.   Help children understand the concept of region by selecting other states and defining their regions.

4.   Identify five regions in the United States (Northwest, Southwest, Midwest, Northeast, Southeast).
     Note: Use the following table to associate particular states with regions:

Northwest	Southwest	Midwest	Northeast	Southeast
Washington	California	North Dakota	Michigan	Arkansas
Oregon	Nevada	South Dakota	Ohio	Louisiana
Idaho	Utah	Nebraska	Pennsylvania	Kentucky
Montana	Arizona	Kansas	New York	Tennessee
Wyoming	Colorado	Missouri	Vermont	Mississippi
	New Mexico	Iowa	Maine	Alabama
	Oklahoma	Minnesota	New Hampshire	Florida
	Texas	Wisconsin	Massachusetts	Georgia
		Illinois	Rhode Island	South Carolina
		Indiana	Connecticut	North Carolina
			New Jersey	Virginia
			Delaware	
			West Virginia	
			Maryland	

5.   Tell pupils they will use soap-dough to make colorful regional maps of the United States.

Major Instructional Sequence:
1.   Form five groups to represent each of the regions. Have each group decide on a color to use for their region.
2.   Assemble materials at group workstations. Have pupils mix the detergent powder and water to a consistency similar to dough. (Make sure the mixture is not too stiff.) Use the food coloring to color the mixture the desired shade.
3.   Help pupils cut the cardboard into the shapes of the six different regions.
4.   Each group places the colored mixture of soap-dough onto the cardboard regions. Labels are placed in the region to identify it as well as individual states in the region.
5.   Let regions dry overnight.

Closure or Evaluation
1.   Once dry, have each group present their region by identifying it and naming the states included in the region.
2.   Have the groups assemble their regions like a jigsaw puzzle to form a map of the United States.
3.   Place regional maps in a learning center for future use.

Topic: LOCATING THE STATES

Grade Level: 3-6   **Activity Time:** 1 class period

Materials Needed:
1. map of United States with states (copy the one above)
2. coloring pencils
3. large political reference map of the United States (wall or spring-roller type)

Objectives:
    As a result of this activity, the learner will:
•   develop a better understanding of where various states in the United States are located.
•   find which states lie on the border.
•   find which states lie in the interior.

Introduction:
1. Using the wall map, point out the following examples of information about state locations:
   - Notice that Louisiana borders the Gulf of Mexico. (Have several pupils come to the map and point to Louisiana and the Gulf of Mexico.)
   - See that Kansas is landlocked, no coast lines. (Have several pupils come to the map and point out Kansas and its surroundings.)
   - Notice that Florida borders both the Atlantic Ocean and the Gulf of Mexico. (Have several pupils come to the map and point out Florida, the Atlantic Ocean, and the Gulf of Mexico.)

Major Instructional Sequence:
1. Give each pupil a copy of the U. S. map with states identified.
2. Direct pupils to listen carefully and use the coloring pencils to follow your directions. Give the following directions, pausing after each to allow time for its completion:
   - Color states blue if they border Canada.
   - Color states yellow if they border the Gulf of Mexico.
   - Color states green if they border the Atlantic Ocean.
   - Color any state red if it touches Illinois.
   - If any state touches the Pacific Ocean and is not already colored, color it brown.
   - Color states which border Mexico orange unless they have already been colored.
3. Draw a square box at the bottom of the page and create a legend or key telling what the various colors mean. (Circulate, check for understanding, and give assistance when needed.)

Closure or Evaluation
1. Let each pupils show and tell about their maps.
2. Display maps in the classroom.

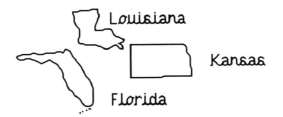

Topic: MAKING PAPIER-MACHÉ GLOBES

Grade Level: 3–6   **Activity Time:** 2 or 3 days

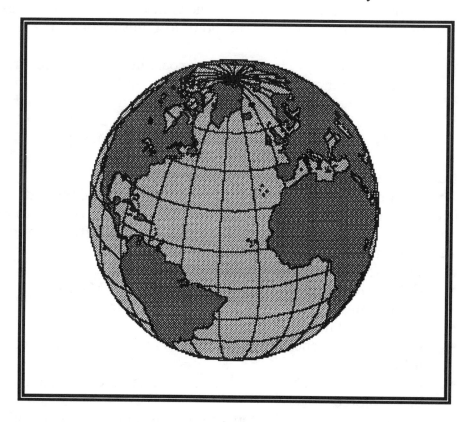

Materials Needed:
  1.   strips of newsprint paper measuring about 10" X 12".
  2.   liquid starch
  3.   tempera paints in assorted colors (especially blue, green, and brown) and brushes
  4.   balloons (durable and spherical, such as "punch-ball" type, 12 to 16 inches in diameter when inflated)

Objectives:
  As a result of this activity, the learner will:
  •   produce a papier-maché globe.
  •   paint the globe to indicate land and water areas (continents and oceans).
  •   label continents and oceans.
  •   (optional) draw, color, and label some countries and regions.

Introduction:
1.   Show and discuss a 16-inch globe.
2.   Call attention to its shape, not round like a penny or nickel but shaped like a ball (spherical).
3.   Pass globe around; let pupils point out land areas and water areas.
4.   Show a model of a papier-maché globe (made earlier by teacher or previous class).
5.   Tell pupils they will begin an activity to make their own papier-maché globes.

Major Instructional Sequence:
1.   Have pupils inflate balloons. (Small children may need teacher's help.)
2.   Assemble paper strips and containers of liquid starch at work areas.
3.   Demonstrate how to dip paper strips in starch and lay in layers on balloon.
4.   After pupils have covered balloons with several layers, let dry overnight.
5.   Assemble tempera paints at work areas.
6.   Have pupils paint continents, oceans, etc. on their hardened papier-maché globes.

Closure or Evaluation
1.   Let pupils show and tell about their individual papier-maché globes.
2.   Have pupils display globes by hanging by a string from the ceiling.

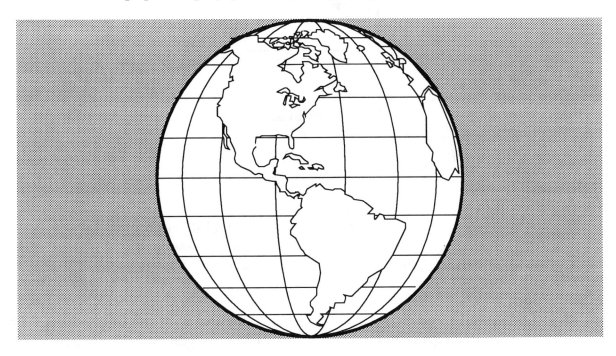

Topic: EARTH'S TILT & REVOLUTION = SEASONS

Grade Level: 3-6   **Activity Time:** 1 class period

Materials Needed:
1. cradle-mounted 16" globe
2. light source which radiates light in all directions (lantern, naked light bulb in a socket, etc.)
3. drawing paper, coloring pencils, crayons

Objectives:
    As a result of this activity, the learner will:
    •   relate seasons to the Earth's tilt and revolution around the sun.
    •   understand that tilt alone does not cause seasons.
    •   understand that revolution alone does not cause seasons.

Introduction:
1. Let a pupil stand in the middle of the room and hold the light source. The light source represents the sun. (Let various pupils have the experience of

holding the light source as the activity continues.)
2.   Demonstrate how the Earth is tilted 23.5° and revolves (orbits) around the sun (light source). Show that the tilt is always in the same direction.
3.   Have different pupils hold the globe (Earth), tilt it on its axis, and revolve (orbit) around the sun (light source). Important: Keep tilt same direction!

Major Instructional Sequence:
1.   As pupils move the Earth (globe) in orbit around the sun (light source), let different pupils identify the position of the Earth to the sun when we have winter. (Check for understanding and make sure that everyone sees that the tilt is away from the sun in the winter.)
2.   As pupils move the Earth (globe) in orbit around the sun (light source), let different pupils identify the position of the Earth to the sun when we have summer; then identify fall and spring in the same way.

Closure or Evaluation
1.   Ask pupils to make a drawing showing the sun and the four positions of the Earth (tilted) during (1) winter, (2) spring, (3) summer, and (4) fall.
2.   Have pupils show and explain their drawings.
3.   Hang drawings on display in the classroom.

Topic: FINDING MOUNTAINOUS AREAS OF THE WORLD

Grade Level: 4-6   **Activity Time:** 1 class period

Materials Needed:
1.   globe (physical-political)
2.   large wall map (physical-political)
3.   atlases, encyclopedias, picture dictionaries, informational books

Objectives:
As a result of this activity, the learner will:
- interpret map legends.
- find mountainous areas of world using map legends.
- find and list information about specific mountainous areas.
- illustrate a mountainous area of the world.

Introduction:
1.   Show pictures and posters (if available) of mountainous areas of the world and discuss their locations (using globe and wall map).
2.   Have pupils gather around the wall map and show them how to determine elevation on the legend. Relate the elevation scale to the mountainous areas shown on the map.
3.   Practice using the legend by having the pupils find and point to

mountainous areas on various continents.

Major Instructional Sequence:
1. Divide pupils into five cooperative work groups.
2. Assign each group one of the following continents: North America, South America, Africa, Europe, or Asia.
3. Each group is to use the globe, maps, and atlases to find as many mountainous areas as possible on their continents.
4. Each group is responsible for getting some basic information about each of the mountainous areas identified from the resources on hand; for example, names of countries, cities, rivers, landmarks, and the like, and information about the people and cultures of the area.
5. Each group is responsible for illustrating one or more of the mountainous areas identified.
6. Circulate, check for understanding, and give assistance when needed.

Closure or Evaluation
1. Each group points out on the wall map and globe the mountainous areas it identified, presents its factual data, and shows its illustration. Have groups plan so that all pupils in the group participate in the presentation.
2. Display reports and illustrations on bulletin board.

Topic: SODA-BOTTLE MAP PROJECTIONS

Grade Level: 5-6   **Activity Time:** 2-3 days

Materials Needed:
1. five plastic soda bottles (1- or 2-liter size)
2. five flashlights
3. five protractors
4. tracing paper
5. marking pens
6. scissors

Objectives:
As a result of this activity, the learner will:
- produce a half-globe by cutting off the top of a plastic soda bottle.
- draw circles inside the half-globe to act as lines of latitude.
- draw radiating spokes to act as lines of longitude.
- produce a planar projection.
- produce a cylindrical projection.
- produce a conical projection.

Introduction:
1. Show and discuss a sixteen-inch globe.
2. Talk about the size and how impractical it would be to carry it around.
3. Show and discuss flat maps. Point out the distortions on a flat map as compared to the globe. (Greenland's size and shape, for example.)
4. Discuss the importance of using the crisscrossing lines of latitude and longitude (technically known as the Earth's geographic graticule or grid system) to find correct locations.
5. Tell pupils they will make a half-globe and practice making map projections.

Major Instructional Sequence:
1. Divide pupils into five cooperative groups and equip each work station with a supply of materials.
2. Have pupils neatly cut off the tops of the plastic soda bottles. Then cut off the bottle-necks as cleanly as possible.
3. Pupils in each group work together cooperatively to:
   - lay the bottle-half on its side and rotate slowly while using the protractor and a pencil to draw circles inside the half-globe to act as lines of latitude.

- draw radiating spokes to act as lines of longitude.
- shine a flashlight at the center of the half-globe while resting it on a sheet of paper, open side up. Lines of latitude and longitude will project onto the paper. This is a planar (flat) projection.
4. Have pupils roll a tube of tracing paper around the half-globe. By shining the flashlight in the middle of the half-globe, the lines of latitude and longitude produce a cylindrical projection. (The lines can be seen through the thin paper.)
5. Have pupils form the tracing paper into a cone and then rest the cone of tracing paper over the polar-end (closed end) of the half-globe. While holding the flashlight in the center, the pupils observe a conical projection through the tracing paper.

Closure or Evaluation
1. Let pupils take turns demonstrating and telling about the projections.
2. Have pupils trace the lines projected onto the tracing paper and display their projections.

Topic: THE CHANGING CONTINENTS

Grade Level: 5-6   **Activity Time:** 1 class period

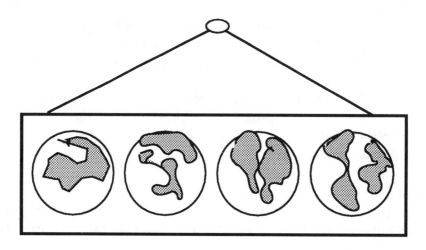

Materials Needed:
1.   styrofoam balls (8 inches in diameter, 20 needed)
2.   fine tip marking pens
3.   regular marking pens
4.   5 sheets of poster board (3′ X 2′)
5.   books, magazines, encyclopedias, pictured dictionaries (such as the *Dorling Kindersley Ultimate Visual Dictionary* published by Dorling Kindersley Publishing, Inc., 95 Madison Avenue, New York, NY 10016).

Objectives:
  As a result of this activity, the learner will:
  •   create globes showing the various stages of continental drift across time.
  •   mount the globes on poster board and label for display.

Introduction:
1.   Using a sixteen-inch globe to demonstrate, explain to pupils that the Earth's crust is the solid outer shell of the Earth. It includes continental crust, which is about twenty-five miles thick, and oceanic crust, which is about four miles thick.
2.   Show how the continents of South America and Africa appear to fit together like the parts of a jigsaw puzzle.
3.   Explain that the continents drift slowly over time and that scientists think the seven continents that we have today were formed from one or more

huge continents in the past.

4. Show pictures and print descriptions from the resources available which depict the changing nature of the shapes and sizes of the Earth's continents over time.
5. Tell pupils they are going to make models of the Earth in various stages of continental drift.

Major Instructional Sequence:

1. Divide pupils into five cooperative work groups.
2. Pupils work cooperatively to research and explore the print materials and pictures available to find four distinct stages of how the Earth's continents appeared at different stages in geologic time.
3. Each group uses four of the styrofoam balls to make models of how the Earth's land areas looked at the different periods.
4. Pupils label the poster board with the descriptions of the four continental appearances of the Earth and glue the styrofoam globes they have made to the poster board over the appropriate labels.

Closure or Evaluation

1. Have each group show and tell about its continental drift globe chart.
2. Display in the classroom or in a school exhibit area.

HISTORY

ACTIVITIES

HISTORY ACTIVITIES

Introduction[1]

History might be defined as the description and interpretation of significant past events. In the elementary school, history is a broadly integrative field, recounting and analyzing human aspirations and strivings in at least five spheres of human activity: social, scientific/technological, economic, political, and cultural (the religious/philosophical/aesthetic). Introducing young children to history — the history of families, their communities, their state, their nation, and various cultures of the world — at once engages them in the lives, aspirations, struggles, accomplishments, and failures of real people, in all these aspects of their lives.

Through history,
•   children come to deeper understandings of society: of different and changing patterns of family structures, of men's and women' roles, of childhood and of children's roles, of various groups in society, and of relationships among all these individuals and groups.

•   children come to deeper understandings of the scientific quest to understand the world in which we live and the quest to do better, or more efficiently, everything from producing food to caring for the ill, to transporting goods, to advancing economic security and the well-being of the group. Understandings of the work people have done, the exchange relationships they have developed with others, and the scientific/technological developments that have propelled change are all central to the study of history and of great interest to children.

•   children come to a beginning understanding of the political sphere of activity as it has developed in their local community, their state, and their nation. Particularly important are understandings of the core principles and values of American democracy that unite us as a people; the people and events that have exemplified these principles in local, state, and national history; and the struggles to bring the rights guaranteed by these principles to all Americans.

•   children come to see that ideas, beliefs, and values have profoundly influenced human actions across time. Religion, philosophy, art, and popular

---

[1] Adapted from Stockard, J., & Wolfinger, D. (in press). *Social studies for the elementary school child: An interdisciplinary approach.* Needham Heights, MA: Allyn & Bacon.

culture have all been central to the aspirations and achievements of all societies and have been a mainspring of historical change from earliest times. Children's explorations of this sphere of human activity, through delving into the literature, sacred writings and oral traditions, drama, art, architecture, music, and dance of a people, bring history to life for children, foster empathy, and deepen their understandings of the human experience.

The Bradley Commission on History in Schools suggested three curricular options for consideration by elementary teachers:

1.   A "here — there — then" approach: This approach first centers instruction in the child's immediate present and then, each year, reaches out in space and back in time to enlarge children's breadth of geographic and historical understandings to distant places and times long ago. From kindergarten onward, this model introduces children to peoples and cultures throughout the world and to historical times as distant as the earliest human memories, contained in myths, legends, and heroic tales, which are part of the cultural heritage of the world.

2.   A modification of the "expanding environments" approach to social studies: This approach includes, each year, rich studies in history and literature that connect with grade-one studies of the family, grade-two studies of the neighborhood, grade-three studies of the community, grade-four studies of the state, grade-five studies of the nation, and grade-six studies of the world, but that expand and deepen these studies far beyond their traditional emphasis on the "here and now." This modified model compares family, community, and state today with family life long ago and with the people and events of earlier times in the historical development of their community and state. This model also compares family and community life in the United States with life in the many cultures from which our increasingly diverse population has come and with the historical experiences and traditions that are part of those cultures.

3.   A "literature-centered" approach: This approach focuses instruction each year on compelling selections of literature from many historical periods which is appropriate for children, and then expands those studies to explore more deeply the historical times they bring to life. This pattern is, essentially, a child's version of the humanities-centered "Great Books" approach to curriculum making, with literature used to take children into adventurous and deeply engaging excursions through a variety of historical eras and cultures.

In 1994, the National History Standards Project released national standards in history in three volumes: *National Standards for History for Grades K-4:*

Expanding Children's World in Time and Space (for grades K-4); *National Standards for United States History: Exploring the American Experience* (for grades 5-12); and *National Standards for World History: Exploring Paths to the Present* (for grades 5-12). These publications are available from the National Center for History in the Schools, UCLA, 10880 Wilshire Boulevard, Suite 761, Los Angeles, CA 90024-4108. The history standards for grades K-4 include:

Living and Working Together in Families and Communities, Now and Long Ago

- Pupils should understand family life now and in the recent past, family life in various places long ago.
- Pupils should understand the history of their local community and how communities in North America varied long ago.

The History of the Pupil's Own State and Region

- Pupils should understand the people, events, problems, and ideas that created the history of their own state.

The History of the United States: Democratic Principles and Values and the People from Many Cultures Who Contributed to Its Cultural, Economic, and Political Thinking

- Pupils should understand how democratic values came to be, and how they have been exemplified by people, events, and symbols.
- Pupils should understand the causes and nature of various movements of large groups of people into and within the United States, now and long ago.
- Pupils should understand regional folklore and cultural contributions that helped to form our national heritage.

The History of Peoples of Many Cultures around the World

- Pupils should understand selected attributes and historical developments of various societies in Africa, the Americas, Asia, and Europe.
- Pupils should understand the major discoveries in science and technology, their social and economic effects, and the scientists and inventors from many groups and regions responsible for them.

History, properly developed for children in the early years of schooling, can open important opportunities to analyze and develop appreciation for all spheres of human activity and of the interactions among them. History gives an appreciation, insight, and understanding of modern problems. Children should be engaged in active questioning and learning and not in the passive absorption of facts, names, and dates. Real historical understanding requires that pupils engage in historical reasoning; listen to and read historical stories, narratives, and literature with meaning; think through cause-effect relationships; interview "old timers" in the community for an oral account of personal and community history; analyze primary source documents, photos, historical newspapers, and the records of the past available in libraries, local museums and historical sites; and construct time-lines and historical narratives of their own. These processes of active learning are essential to developing historical insights and lasting learning. (Note: For excellent sources of historical fiction, nonfiction, and literature, see "Notable Children's Trade Books in the Field of Social Studies," which is published each year in the April/May issue of *Social Education,* the official publication of the National Council for the Social Studies.)

Topic: MAKING CANDLES

Grade Level: 2-3   **Activity Time:** 1 or 2 days

Materials Needed:
1.   pencils and scissors
2.   pieces of string (approximately 6" long)
3.   empty egg cartons, paraffin wax
4.   metal cooking pot (about 1-quart size), electric burner (hot plate)

Objectives:
   As a result of this activity, the learner will:
   •   produce a candle.
   •   understand and appreciate how people functioned before electricity was available.

Introduction:
1.   Show the pupils a few candles of different types.
2.   Let pupils pass the candles around and examine them. Discuss what candles might be used for.
3.   Discuss how candles were used for light before electric light bulbs were invented.
4.   Tell pupils they are going to make candles like people made them in the days before electric light bulbs.

Major Instructional Sequence:
1.   Divide pupils into cooperative work groups (four or five groups).
2.   Assemble materials at group workstations, enough for each pupil in the group to make a candle.
3.   Have pupils tie one end of the wick (string) around the pencil.
4.   Have pupils place the end of the wick that is not tied around the pencil into the bottom of an empty egg carton (one string per cup).
5.   Melt the parafin wax in the metal pot over the electric burner.
6.   Pour the melted wax into the egg carton's cups. (Melt more wax if needed.)
7.   After the wax dries, have pupils cut the wicks (removing pencils).

Closure or Evaluation
1.   Darken room and light candles. Discuss pros and cons of electric lighting and using candles for light.

Topic: CONSTRUCTING A TRANSPORTATION CHART

Grade Level: 2-4   **Activity Time:** 1 class period

Materials Needed:
1.   old magazines, newspapers, catalogs, and a few archival pictures of modes of transportation from long ago to modern times
2.   poster board (6 sheets; 2' X 3')
3.   marking pens
4.   scissors, paste

Objectives:
   As a result of this activity, the learner will:
   •   interpret and display information in graphic form.
   •   create a chart to display modes of transportation used to move people now and long ago.
   •   work cooperatively in groups.

Introduction:
1.   Show pictures of modes of transportation from long ago, such as covered wagons, stage coaches, horse drawn carriages, riders on horseback, longboats with rows of oarsmen, sailing vessels, and the like. Encourage

discussion about why these modes of transportation were in use long ago.

2. Show pictures which fall between long-ago modes (shown in #1 above) and modern modes of transportation, such as early automobiles, steam locomotives, steamships, the first airplanes, and the like. Lead discussion on the advancements made in modes of transportation and why these advancements occurred.
3. Show pictures of modes of transportation which are modern, such as new automobiles, trucks, diesel locomotives, motorboats, nuclear-powered ships, jet airplanes, and the like.

Major Instructional Sequence:
1. Divide pupils into six cooperative work groups.
2. Make two columns on the chalkboard and mark one "LONG AGO" and one "NOW."
3. Have groups make two similar columns on their poster boards.
4. Groups work cooperatively together to search through the magazines, newspapers, catalogs, etc., to find pictures of different modes of transportation.
5. Pupils cut out pictures and paste them on the poster board under the appropriate heading, LONG AGO or NOW.
6. Circulate among groups, checking for understanding and giving assistance when needed.

Closure or Evaluation
1. Groups show and tell about their posters, identifying the modes of transportation, and whether they are from LONG AGO or NOW. (Make sure all pupils in the group have an opportunity to participate in the group's presentation.)
2. Posters are hung for display around the room or in a school exhibit area.

Topic: SCULPTING THE STATUE OF LIBERTY

Grade Level: 3-6   **Activity Time:** 2 days

Emma Lazarus wrote the following poem, "The New Colossus," which is located on the pedestal of the Statue of Liberty:

Give me your tired,
your poor, your huddled masses,
yearning to breathe free,
the wretched refuse of your teeming shore.
Send these, the homeless,
tempest-tossed to me,
I lift my lamp
beside the golden door.

Materials Needed:
1. modeling clay, wax paper, plastic spoons, forks, knives (for sculpting)
2. notebook paper, pencils
3. informational books, history books, and reference materials such as pictured encyclopedias and picture dictionaries

Objectives:
As a result of this activity, the learner will:
- sculpt a model of the Statue of Liberty.
- understand the significance and history of the Statue of Liberty.

Introduction:
1. Use the following background information to give pupils a short overview:
   The Statue of Liberty
   One of the most famous landmarks in the world, the Statue of Liberty overlooks New York Harbor. Originally conceived as a gift from the French to the American

people to honor the 1876 centennial celebration, the 46 m (150.9 ft) high statue was unveiled in 1886. The funds for the statue were donated by the French people and those for the base were raised in the United States. The Statue of Liberty is probably the best-known symbolic image of America.
2. Tell pupils they will use modeling clay to sculpt a replica of the Statue of Liberty.

Major Instructional Sequence:
1. Before they start their sculpting work with the clay, have pupils explore the informational books, history books, and reference materials to find information about the Statue of Liberty.
2. Give each pupil a supply of modeling clay, some waxed paper (on which to work) and some plastic implements (knives, forks, spoons, toothpicks, etc.) with which to sculpt.

Closure or Evaluation
1. Pupils show and tell about their sculptures.
2. Place the sculptures on display in the classroom.

Topic: INDEPENDENCE DAY (FOURTH OF JULY)

Grade Level: 3-6   Activity Time: 2 days

Materials Needed:
   1.   drawing paper, pencils, crayons, coloring pencils
   2.   informational books, history books, and reference materials such as
        pictured encyclopedias and picture dictionaries
   3.   pictures, slides, or filmstrips depicting Independence Day

Objectives:
   As a result of this activity, the learner will:
      •   understand the significance of the Fourth of July in America.
      •   produce an original drawing depicting a Fourth of July activity.

Introduction:
   1.   Use the following background information to give pupils a short
        overview of Independence Day in America:

Independence Day

The most important national holiday in the United States is Independence Day, July 4, which celebrates the adoption of the Declaration of Independence by the Second Continental Congress on July 4, 1776. The day has always been the celebrated with parades, patriotic speeches, picnics, and every variety of noisy jubilation. In fact, the firing of cannon and fireworks caused so many injuries that, by the early 1900s, ordinances forbidding private fireworks were passed in many cities. Today, Fourth of July fireworks are largely handled by professionals.

Major Instructional Sequence:

1. Have pupils use the informational books, history books, and reference materials to find as much information as possible about Independence Day in America.
2. After doing their research, pupils are to draw an original Fourth of July scene on the art paper.
3. Circulate, check for understanding, and give assistance when needed.

Closure or Evaluation

1. Pupils show and tell about their drawings.
2. Place the drawings on the bulletin board.

Topic: MAKING A HORNBOOK

Grade Level: 3-6   **Activity Time:** 1 class period

Materials Needed:
1. cardboard sheets measuring about 12" X 18" (1 per pupil)
2. marking pens in black or brown, beige construction paper, glue
3. clear plastic wrap
4. books with pictures of colonial classrooms and hornbooks

Objectives:
As a result of this activity, the learner will:
- produce a representation of a hornbook.
- create an original poem or short segment of writing to go on the hornbook.
- use the hornbook to simulate learning in a colonial schoolroom.

Introduction:
1. Show pictures of colonial classrooms with hornbooks in use. Show closeup of a hornbook. Let pupils examine photographs closely.
2. Tell pupils that early schools in colonial America used the thin outer cover of a cow's horn to cover the reading material on a small board with a handle, thus the name "Horn Book." Reading and writing material was scarce, and the thin, transparent horn protected the material which was mounted on the board.
3. Tell pupils they will make a simulated hornbook out of cardboard.

Major Instructional Sequence:
1. Have pupils write their original poems or short segments of writing on a sheet of notebook paper. Circulate and give assistance as needed.
2. Show pupils steps in constructing the hornbook:
   - Cut cardboard into the shape of hornbook (rectangular at top with handle for child to hold).
   - Cut construction paper to fit top of cardboard hornbook
   - neatly copy poem or writing onto construction paper.
   - Glue construction paper to cardboard hornbook.
   - Cover with clear plastic wrap.
3. Circulate and give assistance as pupils construct hornbooks.

Closure or Evaluation
1. Have pupils show their hornbooks and share their writings with the class.

Topic: PUZZLE PAIRS

Grade Level: 3-6   **Activity Time:** 1 class period

Materials Needed:
1.   strips of white cardboard about 10" X 3"
2.   felt-tip marking pens, scissors
3.   large paper bag
4.   4 or 5 lists of categories comprised of two-word "pairs," such as
      explorers/explorations, capitals/states, arabic numerals/Roman numerals,
      discoverers/discoverys, countries/continents, cities/countries,
      rivers/continents, and the like

Objectives:
As a result of this activity, the learner will:
   •   interact with other pupils in a cooperative learning environment.
   •   review previously taught information.
   •   match information which has been broken into pairs.

Introduction:
1.   Write Nile River on one card and Africa on another card. Show pupils
      that the match would be "rivers and continents."
2.   Tell pupils they will make groups of matching cards, jumble them
      together in a paper bag, and then work cooperatively to find the matches.

Major Instructional Sequence:
1.   Divide pupils into cooperative work groups (four or five groups).
2.   Assemble materials at group workstations.
3.   Give each group a list of pairs and ask them to write one-half of each
      pairing on a strip of white cardboard.
4.   Collect the cardboard strips in a paper bag.
5.   Have each pupil draw a strip from the paper bag and place it face-down on
      the desk until all have drawn.
6.   Once all pupils have drawn a strip from the bag, let pupils circulate and
      find the person with the matching strip.
7.   After all matches are made, return strips to paper bag, redraw, and do the
      activity again. This may be done several times.

Closure or Evaluation
1.   Let pupils tell about the matches they made: the easiest, the most
      difficult, matches they remember, and why.

Topic: REPLICAS OF ANCIENT ANIMAL-SKIN COATS

Grade Level: 3-6   **Activity Time:** 2 days

Materials Needed:
1.   butcher paper (or large shopping bags)
2.   scissors
3.   tempera paints in assorted colors
4.   crayons
5.   yarn, wool scraps
6.   heavy thread and needle

Objectives:
As a result of this activity, the learner will:
- make a replica of an ancient animal-skin coat.
- realize that some historical and present-day sources of clothing are plants and animals.
- color and paint the coat to resemble fur, skin, down, and the like.

Introduction:
1.   Discuss different historical periods, emphasizing how people used clothing to keep warm.
2.   Explain that skins from wild animals were commonly used for clothing. For example, during the last Ice Age in North America, saber-toothed tiger, bears, large mammoths, and wolves were among the animals hunted for food and clothing. In more recent times, Native American tribes typically hunted elk, deer, buffalo, and seals for meat and clothing.
3.   Explain that when European settlers came to America they brought with them a tradition of making clothing out of linen and wool.
4.   Tell pupils they will participate in an activity to make coats from animal skins like early human groups did.

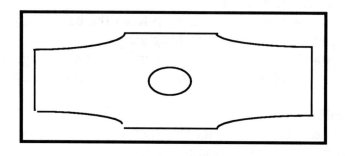

Major Instructional Sequence:
1.   Distribute materials and demonstrate how to draw the illustrated pattern on the butcher paper (or shopping bag) and cut appropriately to make a coat.
2.   Pupils may paint and decorate coats by attaching yarn and wool scraps with glue. Stitch around the borders with the needle and thread to enhance the look.

Closure or Evaluation
1.   Have pupils don their coats and have a "show and tell" fashion show with each pupil modeling and telling about his/her coat.

Topic: DEVELOPING A TIME-LINE OF YOUR LIFETIME

Grade Level: 3-6   **Activity Time:** 1 class period

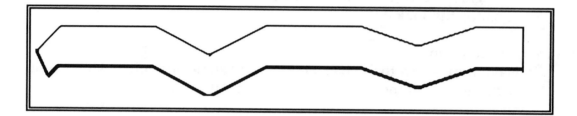

Materials Needed:
1.   long strip of butcher paper (15 to 20 feet long)
2.   paste, scissors, Scotch tape
3.   old magazines, newspapers, catalogs dating back to time of children's birthdays
4.   photographs of pupils and their families at various stages, from when they were babies until the latest photos available
5.   marking pens
6.   miniature time-line of teacher's lifetime (prepared in advance)

Objectives:
As a result of this activity, the learner will:
  • interpret and display historical information in graphic form.
  • work cooperatively with other pupils to develop a large time-line depicting events in pupils' lifetimes.

Introduction:
1.   Demonstrate miniature time-line of teacher's lifetime. Explain that the time-line begins when the teacher was a baby and comes up to the present time. Let pupils examine the time-line closely, looking at the pictures, news clippings, etc., to see that they correlate with different dates and times.

Major Instructional Sequence:
1.   By a show of hands, determine which pupil has the earliest (oldest) birthday and let the pupil mark his/her birth date (day, month, year) on the long strip of butcher paper (time-line).
2.   Continue with the next oldest pupil, etc., until all pupils have recorded their birth dates on the time-line (spaced about five inches apart).

3. Have pupils place subsequent years on the time-line about eighteen inches apart.
4. Pupils Scotch tape their photos under appropriate time periods, placing their earliest baby pictures beneath their birth dates.
5. Pupils search through the old magazines, newspapers, and catalogs to find significant headlines, articles, drawings, cartoons, and photographs to be cut out and pasted on the time-line under the appropriate years.

Closure or Evaluation
1. Each pupil goes to the time-line and explains his/her pictures and contributions.
2. Display the time-line in the classroom. Invite parents and other classes to visit and view the time-line.

Topic: MAKING A DINOSAUR BOOK

Grade Level: 3-6   **Activity Time:** 2 days

Materials Needed:
1. transparency picturing various dinosaurs (use above illustration)
2. drawing paper, construction paper, tagboard
3. scissors, paste
4. collection of books and encyclopedias with information and pictures of dinosaurs

Objectives:
   As a result of this activity, the learner will:
   - work in cooperative groups to create an illustrated book on dinosaurs.
   - develop an interest in dinosaurs and the Earth during dinosaur times.
   - use reference and resource books as tools to seek desired information.

Introduction:
   1. Show the transparency of the dinosaurs. Tell pupils that dinosaurs were reptiles that lived millions of years ago and that some of them were the largest land animals that have ever lived.
   2. Tell them that dinosaurs lived on the Earth for 165 million years but became extinct (no longer existing or living) 65 million years ago.
   3. Let pupils browse through the books and see if they can identify some of the dinosaurs on the overhead transparency.

Major Instructional Sequence:
   1. Divide pupils into six cooperative work groups.
   2. Each group is to create an illustrated book about dinosaurs using the pictures and resources available. A short written description of each dinosaur will be accompanied by an illustration of the dinosaur.
   3. Some popular dinosaurs to look for: Triceratops, Lambeosaurus, Stegosaurus, Brachiosaurus, Plateosaurus, Allosaurus, and Tyrannosaurus.
   4. Circulate among groups, check for understanding, and give assistance when needed.

Closure or Evaluation
   1. Have groups show their dinosaur books and share with the class the pictures and descriptions written about the dinosaurs. Be sure that all group members participate in the oral presentation of the group's work.
   2. Place the dinosaur books in an exhibit on dinosaurs which eventually may include other kinds of artwork.

Topic: GRAVESTONE RUBBINGS

Grade Level: 3-6   **Activity Time:** 2 days

Materials Needed:
1. butcher paper
2. #2 pencils, crayons, charcoal pencils
3. a sample gravestone rubbing (from a previous class or made by teacher)
4. biographies, informational books, history books, and reference materials, such as pictured encyclopedias and picture dictionaries

Objectives:
As a result of this activity, the learner will:
- make a field trip to a local cemetery.
- produce rubbings of gravestones.
- analyze the writings on gravestones.
- produce simulated gravestones of famous persons.

Introduction:
1. Demonstrate a gravestone rubbing.
2. Let pupils examine it carefully.
3. Tell pupils that they will be going on a field trip to a local cemetery.

Major Instructional Sequence:
1. In the cemetery, demonstrate how a gravestone rubbing is made. (Tape a section of butcher paper to the gravestone, then rub the pencil, charcoal pencil, or crayon back and forth across the gravestone so that the image is left on the butcher paper.)
2. Divide pupils into working pairs. Each pair will work together to make

gravestone rubbings, assisting with the taping, holding the paper steady, and doing the rubbing.

3.   Let pupils fan out into the cemetery for a designated time period, then meet back at a central point.

4.   Circulate through cemetery, check for understanding, provide assistance when needed.

Closure or Evaluation

1.   Back in the classroom, share the gravestone rubbings. Let each pair of pupils show and tell about their rubbings.

2.   Pairs work together to create simulated gravestones of famous people who they find in biographies, informational books, history books, and reference materials.

Topic: FOOTPRINT TIME-LINE

Grade Level: 3-6   Activity Time: 1 class period

Materials Needed:
1.   Tagboard or construction paper
2.   Assorted colored markers
3.   Scissors and transparent tape
4.   Magazines and pamphlets representing several years in the past

Objectives:
As a result of this activity, the learner will:
- create a time-line using their own footprints.
- put their time-line in chronological order.
- see that a time-line can picture a time period.

Introduction:
1.   Show and discuss examples of simple time-lines of short duration, such as the time the children have been alive.
2.   Show and discuss time-lines of longer time periods, beginning before the lives of the children in the class.
3.   Demonstrate how time-lines are like a picture of time.

Major Instructional Sequence:
1.   Have pupils trace and cut out their footprints on the tagboard or construction paper.
2.   Each pupil is given a specific year for which to be responsible.
3.   Pupils research the magazines for their year and cut and paste on their footprint an event (including pictures) which occurred during that year.
4.   Pupils place the footprints in chronological order and mount them with tape to the wall, the floor, the chalkboard, a bulletin board, or wherever else they decide is appropriate.

Closure or Evaluation
1.   Have students go to the time-line and talk about the information on their own footprint.
2.   Footprint time-lines can also be made by cooperative groups to represent time periods from history which are discussed in literature, resource materials, textbooks, and other print media.

Topic: SHOE-BOX COLONIES

Grade Level: 4-6   **Activity Time:**   2 to 3 days

Materials Needed:
1.   cardboard
2.   shoe boxes
3.   construction paper & scissors
4.   tempera paint, brushes, felt pens
5.   green butcher paper
6.   glue, clay, craft sticks

Objectives:
As a result of this activity, the learner will:
- construct model plantations of the southern colonies.
- label each colony.
- develop an appreciation for life during plantation times.

Introduction:
1.   Discuss and review life in southern colonies.
2.   Show pictures, filmstrips, models, and the like, of plantation life.

Major Instructional Sequence:
1.   Divide pupils into cooperative work groups (four or five groups).
2.   Assemble materials at group workstations.
3.   Demonstrate how to use the shoe boxes for buildings, cutting roofs for the boxes from the cardboard.
4.   Pupils will paint doors and windows with tempera paint and draw details, such as bricks and wood, with felt pens.
5.   Pupils lay finished buildings out on a table covered with green butcher paper to simulate grass.
6.   Pupils draw and paint paths, trails, ponds, streams, and the like, on the green butcher paper.
7.   For added realism, pupils make miniature wagons, trees, animals, and people from construction paper and clay to include in the display.

Closure or Evaluation
1.   Let groups show and tell about their plantation colonies.
2.   Invite other classes and parents to see the displays.

Topic: MAKING A TIME-LINE OF PRESIDENTS

Grade Level: 3-6   **Activity Time:** 3–4 days

Materials Needed:
1.   long strip of butcher paper (18 to 22 feet long)
2.   paste, scissors, Scotch tape, marking pens
3.   coloring pencils, art paper
4.   list of presidents (next page), encyclopedias, picture dictionaries, informational books, biographies of presidents
5.   transparency of list of presidents (see page 1.44), overhead projector

Objectives:
As a result of this activity, the learner will:
   •   interpret and display historical information in graphic form.
   •   work cooperatively with other pupils to develop a large time-line of the U. S. presidents.
   •   use reference materials to find necessary data for the time-line.
   •   draw pictures of presidents.

Introduction:
1.   Show pictures and talk about various U. S. presidents.
2.   Show transparency of the names and terms of office of the 42 presidents (George Washington through Bill Clinton).

Major Instructional Sequence:

1. Divide pupils into six cooperative work groups. Assign seven presidents to each group.
2. Each group works cooperatively to draw a picture and collect pertinent data for each of their presidents.
3. Picture and data is placed on the time-line at the appropriate place.
4. Groups tell about the data collected on their seven presidents. Groups plan so that all group members participate in the presentation of data.

Closure or Evaluation

1. Time-line is hung on a wall (or walls) of the classroom.
2. Invite other classes and parents to come see the presidential time-line.

PRESIDENTS OF THE UNITED STATES

George Washington
1789-1797

John Adams
1797-1801

Thomas Jefferson
1801-1809

James Madison
1809-1817

James Monroe
1817-1825

John Quincy Adams
1825-1829

Andrew Jackson
1829-1837

Martin Van Buren
1837-1841

William Henry Harrison
March-April, 1841

John Tyler
1841-1845

James K. Polk
1845-1849

Zachary Taylor
1849-1850

Millard Fillmore
1850-1853

Franklin Pierce
1853-1857

James Buchanan
1857-1861

Abraham Lincoln
1861-1865

Andrew Johnson
1865-1869

Ulysses S. Grant
1869-1877

Rutherford B. Hayes
1877-1881

James A. Garfield
Mar.-September, 1881

Chester A. Arthur
1881-1885

Grover Cleveland
1885-1889

Benjamin Harrison
1889-1893

Grover Cleveland
1893-1897

William McKinley
1897-1901

Theodore Roosevelt
1901-1909

William H. Taft
1909-1913

Woodrow Wilson
1913-1921

Warren G. Harding
1921-1923

Calvin Coolidge
1923-1929

Herbert Hoover
1929-1933

Franklin D. Roosevelt
1933-1945

Harry S. Truman
1945-1953

Dwight D. Eisenhower
1953-1961

John F. Kennedy
1961-1963

Lyndon B. Johnson
1963-1969

Richard M. Nixon
1969-1974

Gerald R. Ford
1974-1977

Jimmy Carter
1977-1981

Ronald Reagan
1981-1989

George Bush
1989-1993

Bill Clinton
1993 to date

ANTHROPOLOGY

ACTIVITIES

ANTHROPOLOGY ACTIVITIES

Introduction[1]

Anthropology is often seen as the unifying social science because it is a study of humans, their cultures, how they adapt to their environments, and their growth toward civilization. It is concerned with the development of languages, religions, art, physical and mental traits, and the like. Every society has a culture made up of its beliefs, values, and traditions. Culture is socially learned. People of different cultures have the same psychological and physiological needs but meet their needs based on their culture.

Anthropologists study ways people live in various and diverse cultures, human beings within cultures, and how people interact with culture. They seek knowledge about the customs, laws, traditions, and beliefs of people within a culture and look at physical characteristics, such as race. Looking at the religions of people often leads anthropologists to what may be termed humankind's cultural hearths. Knowledge of both universal and particular traits of the diverse peoples of the world is provided by anthropologists who get most of their information through field studies, where they actually live for prolonged periods within a culture, and from archeological excavations.

Children can develop an appreciation for anthropology and for the work of the anthropologist through skits and simulations where they practice field work within a play-acted culture. Also, simulated digs can be staged with items from our culture buried (planted) by one cooperative group of pupils and excavated by another cooperative group.

---

[1] Adapted from Stockard, J., & Wolfinger, D. (in press). *Social studies for the elementary school child: An interdisciplinary approach.* Needham Heights, MA: Allyn & Bacon.

Topic: MAKING DINOSAUR TRACKS

Grade Level: 1-2   **Activity Time:** 1 class period

Materials Needed:
1. sponges or raw potato halves
2. butcher paper
3. assorted tempera paints
4. shallow trays for paints
5. picture books, well illustrated informational books about dinosaurs, picture dictionaries, and encyclopedias

Objectives:
As a result of this activity, the learner will:
*   practice fine motor skills.
*   enjoy making dinosaur tracks.
*   enhance sensory awareness.
*   develop an awareness of dinosaurs living on the Earth millions of years ago.

Introduction:
1. Tell pupils that dinosaurs were the largest land animals to ever live on the Earth. They disappeared and became extinct (no longer existing or living) about 65 million years ago. Before that, dinosaurs lived on the Earth for some 165 million years.
2. Examine pictures of dinosaurs in picture books, encyclopedias, picture dictionaries, and illustrated informational books. Call attention to the feet of the dinosaurs and let the children draw on the chalkboard how the various footprints of dinosaurs may have looked.
3. Tell children that paleontologists are scientists who study about the past by examining fossils (a remnant or trace of an organism of a past geologic age, such as a skeleton or leaf imprint, embedded and preserved in the Earth's crust). Footprints can be fossils.

4. Tell pupils that the footprints of dinosaurs tell scientists many things about the animal that made them, such as size, speed, and living habits.
5. Tell pupils that they will make their own dinosaur tracks.

Major Instructional Sequence:
1. Set up several work areas around the room with the necessary supplies.
2. Help pupils cut sponges or potato halves into dinosaur footprint shapes. (As a safety factor, teacher does this operation using scissors and/or knife.)
3. Provide each pupil with a section of butcher paper (about three feet long).
4. Pour the pre-mixed tempera paint into the shallow trays. One color may be used in all trays or each tray may have a different color.
5. Show pupils how to dip their sponges (or potato halves) into the paint and carefully press onto the paper to make dinosaur tracks.
6. Pupils sign their tracks and let them dry.

Closure or Evaluation
1. Each person shows and tells about his/her dinosaur tracks. (Some may have a specific dinosaur picture in a book they want to show as a model for their tracks.)
2. Hang the dinosaur tracks on display around the room.

Topic: LOOKING AT FINGERPRINTS

Grade Level: 1-3   **Activity Time:** 3–4 days

Materials Needed:
1. white index cards (unlined, 3" X 5")
2. ink stamp pad
3. liquid soap, paper towels
4. several cleans sheets of white duplicator paper
5. thermal transparencies
6. overhead projector

Objectives:
As a result of this activity, the learner will:
*   discover that each person's fingerprints are different.
*   talk about people's similarities and differences.
*   make personal fingerprint on a card to keep.
*   examine and compare different fingerprints side by side.

Introduction:
1. Place children in pairs facing each other. Ask each pair to look at one another and to note how they are alike and how they are different. (Let everyone tell what they think.)
2. Tell children to look at the tips of their fingers. Tell them that they all have different fingerprints.
3. Tell pupils they will perform an activity to see the differences in their fingerprints.

Major Instructional Sequence:
1. Using the ink pad, the index cards, and the white duplicator paper:
    *   Make each child's right thumbprint on an index card (label with name).
    *   Make each child's right thumbprint on the duplicator paper. Write name of child beneath thumbprint.
    *   Clean each child's thumbs (and hands) with the liquid soap and the paper towels.
2. Make thermal transparencies of the thumbprints on duplicator paper.
3. Display the thumbprints. Let each child examine the screen closely, looking at his/her own thumbprint in relation to the other thumbprints.
4. Lead children in a discussion of how all of the thumbprints are different.

Closure or Evaluation
1. Each pupil attaches a small snapshot to the index card with his/her thumbprint.
2. The index-card thumbprints are displayed on a classroom bulletin board.

Topic: SAND PAINTING

Grade Level: 2-4   **Activity Time:** 1 class period

Materials Needed:
1. salt
2. Ziploc bags
3. food coloring (assorted colors)
4. paper plates
5. glue

Objectives:
As a result of this activity, the learner will:
- produce a sand painting.
- realize that Native American groups, particularly the Navajos, used sand paintings to promote healing.

Introduction:
1. Show a model of a sand painting done previously.
2. Tell children that Native Americans frequently did sand paintings.
3. Relate how the Navajo medicine men used sand paintings to promote healing.
4. Tell pupils that they will make their own sand paintings.

Major Instructional Sequence:
1. Have pupils pour salt into their Ziploc bags (demonstrate and assist, if necessary).
2. Give each pupil a container of a single food coloring.
3. Demonstrate how to add a few drops of food coloring to the salt in the bag, seal the bag, and shake to mix. Allow to dry for a few minutes.
4. While the colored salt is drying in the bags, give each pupil a paper plate.
5. Each pupil creates a design on the paper plate with the glue.
6. Pupils sprinkle different colors of the dyed salt onto the glue to completely cover their design.
7. Have pupils shake the excess salt off the plate. Allow glue to harden. (Circulate, check for understanding, and give assistance when needed all during the sand-painting activity.)

Closure or Evaluation
1. Have pupils show and tell about their finished sand paintings.
2. Display the sand paintings in the classroom or in an exhibit area in the school.

Topic: Making Papier-Maché Pinatas

Grade Level: 3–6   **Activity Time:**   2 or 3 days

Materials Needed:
1.   strips of newsprint and/or butcher paper measuring about 10″ X 2″
2.   liquid starch
3.   assorted colors of tissue paper measuring about 1″ X 6″
4.   baloons of various sizes (party variety)
5.   individually wrapped pieces of candy
6.   butcher paper for work area
7.   paper tape, Exacto knife, and fishing line
8.   broom stick and bandana (for blindfolding)
9.   mexican music, tortilla chips, and salsa dip

Objectives:
As a result of this activity, the learner will:
- produce a papier-maché pinata.
- place the candy pieces inside the pinata.
- attach fishing line to the pinata for hanging.
- break open the pinata and eat the candy.
- enjoy a Mexican fiesta environment.

Introduction:
1.   Play Mexican music softly in the background; let pupils have access to chips and salsa.
2.   Show the pupils a model of a previously made pinata and discuss it as a symbol of celebration (such as birthdays) in Mexico.
3.   Pass pinata so that pupils can examine it more closely.
4.   Tell pupils they will begin an activity to make their own papier-maché pinatas.

Major Instructional Sequence:
1.   Have pupils inflate balloons.
2.   Assemble paper strips and containers of liquid starch at work areas. (Cover work areas with butcher paper.)
3.   Demonstrate how to dip paper strips in starch and apply in layers on balloon.
4.   After pupils have covered balloons with several layers, apply tissues to wet surface so they stick, giving a fluffy, colorful look.
5.   Let pinatas dry overnight.

6. Assemble tape, candy, and fishing line at work areas.
7. Cut small holes in top of pinatas and insert candy pieces; then tape the hole, attaching fishing line with tape in process.

Closure or Evaluation
1. Let pupils show and tell about their individual papier-maché pinatas.
2. Let pupils assist you in hanging pinatas.
3. Let pupils take turns trying to break a pinata with the broomstick while blindfolded.

Topic: MAKING MINIATURE TOTEM POLES

Grade Level: 3–5   **Activity Time:** 1 day

Materials Needed:
1. construction paper
2. glue
3. scissors
4. cardboard tubes (from inside rolls of paper towels)
5. copies of animal descriptions
6. pencils and paper

Objectives:
As a result of this activity, the learner will:
- understand the place of totem poles in Native American culture.
- cut and glue appropriate animal shapes to correspond with story.
- produce a totem pole to represent a story.

Introduction:
1. Show and discuss pictures of totem poles and Native Americans of the Northwest.
2. Explain that the totem pole was a way of recording legends because these Native Americans of the Northwest Coast had no written language.
3. Pass out copies of animal descriptions: Bear = symbol of strength; Beaver = symbol of wealth and gives "medicine power"; Frog = brings good fortune; Raven = guardian spirit; Salmon = symbol of wealth, fertility, and immortality; Snake = brings power of magic; Thunderbird = chief of all guardian spirits and causes thunder and lightning; Whale = bad spirit who brings destruction; Wolf = helpful spirit and also brings skill in weaving and woodcraft.
4. Show a model of a totem pole (made previously by teacher or pupils).
5. Tell pupils they will make their own totem poles.

Major Instructional Sequence:
1. Working in cooperative groups of four to five, have pupils design and sketch totem poles on scratch paper using symbols that will tell a story.
2. Have each group collect and assemble the materials they will need from a central supply table.
3. Coordinate as pupils cut the needed animal shapes from construction paper and cut out features, such as eyes, teeth, claws, etc., from contrasting colors for more dramatic effect.

4. Have pupils glue animals to the cardboard tubes to create a totem pole which tells their story.

Closure or Evaluation
1. Let pupils share their totem poles and tell the stories they depict.
2. Display totem poles on a flat surface where they can be freestanding as an ongoing exhibit.

Topic: MAKING TIME CAPSULES

Grade Level: 3–6   **Activity Time:**   2 or 3 days, culminating at the
end of school.

Materials Needed:
1.   Polaroid camera
2.   drawing paper, manila envelopes, crayons, marking pens
3.   a large box (to serve as a time capsule)
4.   crayons and markers
5.   a pre-made time capsule

Objectives:
As a result of this activity, the learner will:
*   relate to the concept of passing time.
*   undersand that time brings changes.
*   see that the changes brought by time are not something to fear.

Introduction:
1.   Show a pre-made time capsule containing pictures of yourself at
younger ages, old magazine advertisements of cars, appliances,
electronics, and the like, and any other aged items.
2.   Note how your pictures changed with time; how cars, clothes,
appliances, electronics, etc., have changed.
3.   Tell the children that they are going to make their own time capsules.

Major Instructional Sequence:
1.   Take a Polaroid photograph of each child.
2.   Have each child complete individual tasks: write their names, addresses,
and phone numbers in their best possible handwriting; spell the most
difficult word they know; work a difficult math problem; draw a sample of
their best artwork; trace the outline of hands and feet on drawing paper.
Write answers to these questions on a sheet of paper: Favorite color, food,
TV show, entertainer, movie, subject in school, and beverage.
3.   Have each child place his/her photo and materials in a manila envelope,
seal it, sign the outside, and place in the time capsule.
4.   Pupils work cooperatively under teacher's direction to paint and label the
time capsule, seal it securely, and place it in a corner of the room.
5.   Open the time capsule during the last days of the school year.

Closure or Evaluation
1. Let pupils examine and share their envelopes from the time capsule.
2. Have pupils share and discuss the changes they observe.

Topic: MAKING A NATIVE AMERICAN RATTLE

Grade Level: 3-6   **Activity Time:** 1 class period

Materials Needed:
1. aluminum soda-pop can
2. 10" wooden dowel, 1/2 inch in diameter
3. masking tape
4. dry beans
5. construction paper
6. hammer, nail
7. scissors, marking pens

Objectives:
    As a result of this activity, the learner will:
- make a Native American musical instrument (rattle).
- decorate the rattle using construction paper and marking pens.
- develop an understanding and appreciation of the use of rattles in Native American ceremonies.

Introduction:
1. Pass a model rattle around for pupils to examine.
2. Discuss the use and importance of rattles in Native American ceremonies. (Native Americans sometimes used their rattles to accompany musical chants, to round up and corral horses, and in various dances and ceremonies.)
3. Tell pupils they will make their own Native American rattles.

Major Instructional Sequence:
1. Have pupils obtain the necessary materials from the work area.
2. Demonstrate the steps in making the rattle:
   - Insert the dowel into the opening of the can.
   - Secure the dowel with the nail in the top of the can.
   - Insert about fifteen beans into the opening of the can.
   - Tape the opening securely with the masking tape.
   - Cover the can with construction paper.
   - Use the marking pens to decorate the rattle with Native American symbols and designs.
3. Circulate as pupils construct their rattles, check for understanding, and give assistance when needed.

Closure or Evaluation
1. Each pupil shows and demonstrates his/her rattle.
2. Use the rattles in concert to keep time to a chant, or a beat, or a popular song. (Use cassette tape if available.)
3. Make a display of the Native American rattles in the classroom or in a school exhibit area.

Topic: MAKING NATIVE AMERICAN POTTERY

Grade Level: 3-6   **Activity Time:** 2 days

Materials Needed:
1. strips of newsprint (about 10" X 1")
2. liquid starch
3. assorted colors of tempera paints
4. small, plastic "tubs" (such as soft-margarine or cottage cheese tubs)

Objectives:
As a result of this activity, the learner will:
*   produce a replica of Native American pottery.
*   paint the pottery with symbols and colors of particular Native American groups.

Introduction:
1. Show and discuss replicas and pictures of Native American pottery.
2. Let pupils examine the different sizes and designs of the pottery.

Major Instructional Sequence:
1. Lead a discussion of the importance of craftsmanship in Native American culture.
2. Tell pupils they will make their own replicas of Native American pottery.
3. Divide pupils into work groups and assemble paper strips, liquid starch, and plastic butter dishes at group work areas.
4. Demonstrate how to dip the strips into the liquid starch and place in layers over the plastic containers.
5. Once pupils have covered their butter dishes with several layers of strips, allow to dry overnight.
6. Assemble tempera paints and brushes in work areas and have pupils paint designs and symbols onto their pottery. Have pictures and models for ideas.

Closure or Evaluation
1. Pupils display their Native American pottery in a room or school exhibit area.

Topic: MAKING AN AFRICAN RAINSTICK

Grade Level: 3-6   **Activity Time:** 2-3 days

Materials Needed:
1. six large cardboard tubes (2 to 4 feet long, 1 to 3 inches in diameter; a mailing tube, for example), hammer, nails of various sizes
2. tempera paints in black, brown, and red, small plastic bowls
3. plastic knives, small raw potatoes, seeds, beans, rice
4. a sample rainstick (made by a previous class or by the teacher)
5. globe, world map

Objectives:
As a result of this activity, the learner will:
*   produce a cardboard replica of an African rainstick.
*   decorate the rainstick with African designs.
*   demonstrate the use of the rainstick to make sounds.

Introduction:
1. Show a model of a sample rainstick and demonstrate its sounds.
2. Let children examine the rainstick and move it to make sounds.
3. Relate how tribes in Africa use the rainstick to simulate the sound of rain and to make music. Some tribes think it helps bring rain.
4. Tell pupils that they will make their own African rainsticks.

Major Instructional Sequence:
1. Divide pupils into six cooperative work groups and assemble the groups at work stations where the materials are available.
2. Demonstrate and have groups hammer long and short nails into the cardboard tube in a spiral.
3. Cover one end of the tube (use the plastic caps which come with mailing tubes and reinforce with tape) and put rice, seeds, and beans into the tube (one cup of each).

4. Seal the tube by covering the open end.
5. Use the plastic knives to cut the potatoes in half. Carve designs into the flat side of the potato. (Pupils may get ideas from the designs below.)
6. Dip the potatoes into the shallow bowls of tempera paint and stamp the designs onto the rainstick tube.
7. Let rainsticks dry.

Closure or Evaluation
1. Let each group show and demonstrate its rainstick.
2. Place the rainsticks in a classroom exhibit or in a school exhibit area.

Topic: BUILDING A PUEBLO VILLAGE

Grade Level: 3-6   **Activity Time:** 3–4 days

Materials Needed:
1. shoe boxes, brown tempera paint, brushes
2. black construction paper, butcher paper
3. clay, spray glue, craft sticks, sand, small stones, weed clumps
4. model of a Pueblo village (made by teacher or previous class)

Objectives:
As a result of this activity, the learner will:
- construct a model of a Pueblo village.
- make a model of a small clay pot.
- make ladders with craft sticks and spray glue.

Introduction:
1. Gather pupils around the book table and find pictures and items about Pueblo villages.
2. Show the model of the Pueblo village. Let pupils examine the model and the pictures in the books closely. Lead a discussion about what life might have been like in a Pueblo village.
3. Tell pupils that they will construct a model of a Pueblo village.

Major Instructional Sequence:
1. Direct pupils in removing lids from shoe boxes, turning them upside down, and painting them with the brown tempera paint. (Paint over newspapers placed on tables or the floor.)
2. Have pupils make doors and windows from the black construction paper and glue onto the topmost parts of the shoeboxes.
3. Have pupils spray some glue onto the butcher paper and sprinkle sand to simulate desert terrain and add small stones and clumps of vegetation.
4. Have pupils arrange the boxes in a "U" shape on the terrain with the doors and windows facing to the inside of the "U".
5. Direct pupils in making ladders from craft sticks and attaching the ladders with glue so that they lead up to the doors.

Closure or Evaluation
1. Pupils prepare oral presentations about the Pueblo village so they can be guides for visitors who come to see the village (invite other classes and parents). Have all pupils, if possible, participate in acting as guides.

Topic: MAKING MODELS OF EARLY SHIPS AND BOATS

Grade Level: 3-6   **Activity Time:** 2-3 days

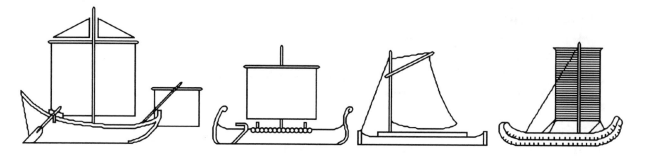

Materials Needed:
1. pictured encyclopedias, picture dictionaries, informational books, filmstrips (if available), posters showing early boats (if available)
2. construction paper, cardboard, tagboard
3. marking pens, coloring pencils, crayons, scissors
4. thread, string, cloth pieces (such as pieces of a sheet, pillow case, etc.)
5. tempera paints, brushes
6. popsicle sticks, craft sticks, glue
7. model boat or ship made by previous class (or by the teacher)

Objectives:
As a result of this activity, the learner will:
*   make a model of an early ship.
*   identify the model ship with a time and a culture.
*   find and list factual information on the time and the culture.
*   participate in a cooperative work group.

Introduction:
1. Show pictures and discuss ships and boats associated with various cultures over time, for example:
    *   Viking longships
    *   Egyptian reed boats
    *   Phoenician trading ships
    *   Arab dhows (traditional Arab sailing boats)
    *   Greek and Roman triremes (sailing ships with lines of rowers for speed)
2. Show the model and let pupils examine it closely.

3.   Tell pupils that they will work in groups to (1) research and find information about early ships and boats, and (2) select a specific boat from which to make a model.

Major Instructional Sequence:
1.   Divide pupils into five cooperative work groups. Each group will work cooperatively in researching information and building their model.
2.   Make materials and supplies available to the groups. Circulate among the groups, check for understanding, and give assistance when needed.

Closure or Evaluation
1.   Each group displays its model and makes an oral presentation about the culture represented by the model. Tell groups to plan so that all group members participate in the oral presentation.
2.   Class votes on (1) the best model and (2) the best presentation.
3.   Groups make informative labels for their models (on large index cards) and put the models on display in the classroom or in a school exhibit area.

Topic: MAKING A PLASTIC SCRIMSHAW

Grade Level: 3-6   **Activity Time:** 1 class period

Materials Needed:
1. large white plastic jugs, one per pupil (such as those used for bleach)
2. pencils, scissors, black crayons, paper
3. paper towels
4. large needle
5. carbon paper
6. picture books on the New England Colonies depicting scrimshaw art, pictured encyclopedias and dictionaries, and similar print resources containing information about the New England Colonies

Objectives:
As a result of this activity, the learner will:
- make a simulation of a scrimshaw (the carving of designs or pictures on the teeth or jawbone of the sperm whale; a popular art form in the New England Colonies).
- have an appreciation for the scrimshaw art form.

Introduction:
1. Tell pupils that artisans in the New England Colonies of the United States carved designs and pictures on the teeth and jawbones of sperm whales to create art.
2. Show pictures and discuss the applicable material in the print resources available.
3. Tell pupils that each of them will create a scrimshaw.

Major Instructional Sequence:
1. Demonstrate how to cut and flatten a smooth piece from the plastic jug.
2. Pupils draw a design or picture on a sheet of paper.
3. Pupils tape their drawings to the back of the carbon paper.
4. Pupils place the carbon paper onto the plastic piece with the drawing facing out.
5. Have pupils trace the drawing onto the plastic piece.
6. Pupils use the long needle to etch their drawings into the plastic.
7. To darken the scratched and etched lines, have pupils rub them lightly with the black crayon.
8. Have pupils clean off the excess crayon with the paper towel.

Closure or Evaluation
1. Take turns showing and telling about individual scrimshaws.
2. Make an exhibit of the scrimshaws in a class location or school exhibit area.
3. Have pupils cooperatively compose a label for the exhibit describing scrimshaws.

Topic: Making a Travel Brochure

Grade Level: 3-6   **Activity Time:** 3 days

Materials Needed:
1.   white construction paper, assorted tempera paint, brushes, glue
2.   various colored markers, assorted magazines, travel brochures, scissors

Objectives:
As a result of this activity, the learner will:
- create a travel brochure as if they were going to use it in a travel agency.
- research factual information about different countries, focusing on climate, location, food, tourist attractions, and scenery.
- work in cooperative groups in a collaborative effort.
- make an oral presentation about the travel brochure as a travel agent might do.

Introduction:
1.   Show and present to the class an actual travel brochure from a travel agency.
2.   Ask if any class members have been to a foreign country; if so, ask them to

tell about it.
3. Tell the class they will be working together in groups to create travel brochures.

Major Instructional Sequence:
1. Divide the class into five cooperative work groups.
2. Assign one of the following countries to each group: Egypt, India, the Netherlands, Mexico, France.
3. Give the groups a period of time to research their country in the library on the first day.
4. In creating the travel brochure, each group will fold the white construction paper into four segments so that the paper is made into a pamphlet that opens up accordion-style.
5. Groups will label the brochure with the country's name and write two to four sentences about each topic addressed. Leave room for pictures which will either be cut from magazines or travel brochures or drawn/painted in by the pupils.

Closure or Evaluation
1. Each group makes a presentation of its brochure, trying to persuade the audience that traveling to their country is a "must." (Make sure that all group members participate in the group presentation of the travel brochure.)
2. Class votes on most influential brochure and presentation.
3. Display travel brochures around the classroom or in a school exhibit area.

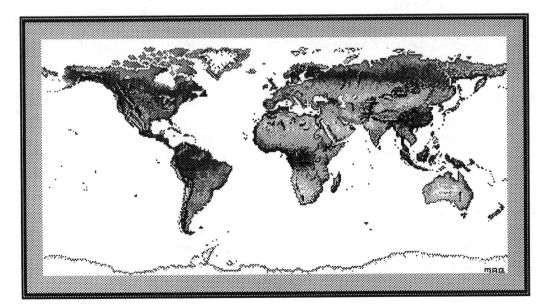

Topic: MAKING A MARACA

Grade Level: 2-3   **Activity Time:** 1 class period

Materials Needed:
1. aluminum cans, spray-painted white, with a 5/16-inch hole drilled in the bottom of the can
2. unsharpened #2 wooden pencils, masking tape
3. tempera paints in assorted colors, brushes, assorted dry beans
4. cassette of the song, "La Bamba"
5. sample maraca (either a real maraca or one made previously)

Objectives:
As a result of this activity, the learner will:
- produce a maraca.
- decorate the maraca using the assorted tempera paints.
- play the maraca along with the tempo of the song, "La Bamba"

Introduction:
1. Show a picture (or models, if available) of maracas.
2. Demonstrate and discuss how the maraca is used (along with the song, "La Bamba."
3. Tell pupils they will make their own maracas and play them to music.

Major Instructional Sequence:
1. Assemble materials at work areas.
2. Pupils paint artwork onto the white spray-painted cans using tempera.
3. Allow cans to dry for ten to fifteen minutes before continuing the construction phase of the activity.
4. Pupils place pencils into the 5/16-inch holes drilled in the bottom of the cans.
5. Have pupils insert ten to fifteen dry beans into the original holes in the tops of their cans and place masking tape over the original holes to prevent the beans from spilling out.

Closure or Evaluation
1. Let pupils show and demonstrate their maracas.
2. Play the recording, "La Bamba," and let the class use their maracas to play along with the tempo of the song.
3. Place the maracas in a classroom exhibit.

SOCIOLOGY

ACTIVITIES

SOCIOLOGY ACTIVITIES

Introduction[1]

Sociology is the study of social institutions, processes, and problems. Sociologists study ways in which people interact with the general society. They examine the social system, particularly the institutions of the social order and the grouping instinct whereby people participate in family groups, church groups, and other social groups. Sociologists look at the structure of society in its groups, sub-groups, social classes, and institutions.

Some key concepts to be developed in sociology include socialization, society, group, role, social control, social class, status, and institution. Major sociological generalizations for the elementary school might include (1) looking at the family as the basic social unit, (2) examining evidence that shows that every society has had social classes, (3) finding that every society develops a system of roles, values, and the like, (4) discovering that all societies develop a system of social control, (5) and understanding that a person's social environment has a profound effect on his personal growth and development.

---

[1] Adapted from Stockard, J., & Wolfinger, D. (in press). *Social studies for the elementary school child: An interdisciplinary approach.* Needham Heights, MA: Allyn & Bacon.

Topic: THE CLOCKS OF TIME

Grade Level: 1-3   **Activity Time:** 1 class period

Materials Needed:
1.   various clocks, watches, and timepieces (brought by children or their parents in response to an earlier request)
2.   newspaper advertisement pages, advertising supplements, catalogs, fliers, magazines, and brochures
3.   poster board (6 sheets, 2' X 3' size)
4.   scissors, paste

Objectives:
As a result of this activity, the learner will:
   •   explore the variety of timepieces used now and long ago.
   •   note the similarities and differences in different kinds of watches and clocks.
   •   appreciate that different kinds of timepieces serve the function of telling what time it is.

Introduction:
1.   Gather children around a table (or tables) where all kinds of watches, clocks, and timepieces are exhibited.
2.   Let children freely handle the watches and clocks and compare them with one another. Encourage discussion.

Major Instructional Sequence:
1.   Divide pupils into six cooperative work groups.
2.   Supply each work group with a poster board, scissors, paste, and a variety of newspaper advertisement pages, advertising supplements, catalogs, fliers, magazines, and brochures.
3.   Each group is to find and cut out pictures of watches, clocks, and timepieces and paste them on their poster board to form a "Clocks of Time" collage.

4.   Circulate among the groups, check for understanding, and give assistance when needed.

Closure or Evaluation
1.   Groups show and tell about their "Clocks of Time" posters (all participate).
2.   Posters are displayed around the room.

Topic: OBSERVING CHANGE

Grade Level: 2-4   **Activity Time:** 3 days

Materials Needed:
1.   children's book, *Mirandy and Brother Wind* by Patricia McKissick, published by Knopf (1988)

Objectives:
As a result of this activity, the learner will:
- describe a family artifact.
- examine old photographs showing grandparents when they were young.
- write stories about artifacts and photographs.

Introduction:
1.   Read *Mirandy and Brother Wind* to the class.
2.   Call attention to the author's note about the photograph of her grandparents before they were married that had inspired the book.
3.   Discuss the terms from the book, "cakewalk" and "conjurer."

Major Instructional Sequence:
1.   Ask, "Do you have any old photographs of your grandparents when they were young?" (Most children will. Encourage them to get their parents' permission to bring the photos the next day.)
2.   Ask, "Do you have anything that was owned by your parents or grandparents when they were young?" (Most children will. Encourage them to get their parents' permission to bring these "artifacts" the next day. Items such as carved wooden eggs, ancient waffle irons, handcrafted salt and pepper shakers, newspapers, cooking utensils, old photographs, and the like, are examples of what to expect.)
3.   Tell pupils to be sure to ask their parents about the story that goes along with the artifact they bring.

4. The next day, pupils show and tell about their grandparents' photographs and their artifacts.
5. They label and make a display of the artifacts and photographs.

Closure or Evaluation
1. Pupils write stories about each artifact. When the stories are revised and edited by peers, they are bound into a classroom book along with pictures drawn by the pupils to go with the stories.

Topic: MAKING A MURAL OF HOUSE TYPES

Grade Level: 2-6　　　　　　　　　　**Activity Time:** 1 class period

Materials Needed:
1.　magazines
2.　marking pens
3.　large (3' X 2') poster board (5 needed)
4.　scissors
5.　paste

Objectives:
　As a result of this activity, the learner will:
　　•　develop an awareness of different types of houses.
　　•　work cooperatively to create a mural of house types.

Introduction:
1.　Lead pupils in a discussion of various kinds of houses in which people live.
2.　List different types of houses mentioned by pupils on chalkboard, such as:
　　•　ranch-style houses　　　　•　two-story houses
　　•　apartment houses　　　　•　mobile homes
　　•　duplexes　　　　　　　　•　condominiums
　　•　high-rise buildings　　　　•　town houses
　　•　house boats　　　　　　　•　mansions
3.　Let pupils describe their own house types.
4.　Show a mural of house types (done by previous class or by teacher)

Major Instructional Sequence:
1. Divide pupils into five cooperative work groups.
2. Pupils search through magazines for pictures of different house types.
3. Pupils cut out pictures and paste onto the poster board to form a mural of house types.
4. Optional (depending on grade level): have pupils make labels for the different house types.

Closure or Evaluation
1. Have each group show and tell about its mural on house types. (Help the groups plan their presentations so that each group member has a part in the presentation.)
2. Make an exhibit of the house types to be placed in a class location or in a school exhibit area.

Topic: DISTINGUISHING BETWEEN RURAL AND URBAN

Grade Level: 2-6   **Activity Time:** 1 class period

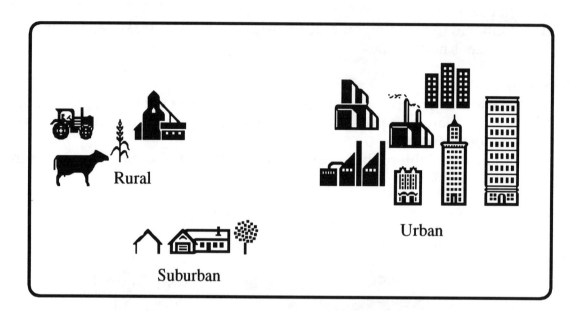

Materials Needed:
1.   state highway maps (6)
2.   transparency (previously made with two column headings: RURAL and URBAN)
3.   Six sheets of poster board (about 2' X 3')
4.   pencils, notebook paper

Objectives:
   As a result of this activity, the learner will:
   •   distinguish between rural and urban communities.
   •   identify rural and urban communities on a state map.
   •   list rural and urban communities in specific counties.

Introduction:
1.   Use the overhead to show the transparency with the two column headings, RURAL and URBAN.
2.   Divide pupils into six cooperative work groups and give each group a state highway map and a sheet of poster board.
3.   Let pupils help you find the state's largest city. Contrast it with some of

the smaller towns in the same county or adjacent counties. Define the largest city in the state as an urban setting and the smaller towns in the state as rural settings.

4. Brainstorm with pupils about characteristics of an urban setting and characteristics of a rural setting (jobs, transportation, etc.) {Note that rural towns are not just small but are usually isolated from larger cities.}

Major Instructional Sequence:

1. Assign to each group several specific counties in the state.
2. Ask each group to identify urban cities and rural towns in the counties assigned to them.
3. Have each group identify the number of Interstate Highways in each county assigned, the number of Federal Highways, the number of State Highways, the number of County Highways and Farm Roads.
4. Ask each group to make a RURAL column and an URBAN column on the poster board and record their data.

Closure or Evaluation

1. Let groups show and tell about their posters. Be sure that all group members participate in the presentation.
2. Call attention to unusual findings such as counties with only county highways and farm roads, counties with only rural towns, and the like.
3. Hang the rural/urban posters around the room.

Topic: MAKING PASSPORTS

Grade Level: 3-6   **Activity Time:** 1 class period

Materials Needed:

1. resource books such as encyclopedias, atlases, informational books, *National Geographic Magazine,* etc., containing information about various countries of the world
2. globes and political maps of the world
3. duplicator paper (8 1/2" X 11") cut into quarters (each single sheet makes 4 pages)
4. construction paper, hole-punch (plier-type), and brads
5. notebook paper, pencils, marking pens
6. a copy of a real passport (teacher's own, borrowed from someone, or obtained from the U. S. government passport office located in most large post offices)

Objectives:

As a result of this activity, the learner will:

- produce a simulated passport for travel to several countries.
- research basic information about the countries listed in the passport.
- increase knowledge about countries of the world.

Introduction:

1. On the globe and world political map, point out several countries to which one might choose to travel. Lead pupils in related discussion.
2. Discuss the necessity of obtaining a passport in order to travel from one country to another. Lead pupils in related discussion.
3. Show the passport and identify its various components. Pass around for pupils to examine closely.

Major Instructional Sequence:

1. Tell pupils they will select at least three countries but no more than seven, research information about the countries in the resources available, and construct a passport showing they have traveled to each of the countries selected. (Demonstrate how to use the small, quartered-sheets of duplicator paper as pages for the passport and the construction paper for the front and back covers, and punch holes and use brads to bind the passport.)
2. Tell pupils that when it comes time to share the passports, they will also give information about each of the countries, information that would be important to a visitor.
3. As pupils work on their passports, circulate, check for understanding, and give assistance when needed.

Closure or Evaluation

1. Each pupil shows his/her passport and gives pertinent information about the countries included.
2. Pupils vote on the most authentic passport.
3. Pupils vote on the most interesting report.
4. Passports are displayed on a special bulletin board.

Topic: MAKING A MARDI GRAS KING CAKE

Grade Level: 3-6

Activity Time: 2 days

Louisiana

Materials Needed:

1. 3 cups of flour
2. 1 teaspoon salt
3. 1/4 cup warm water
4. 3/4 cup scalded milk
5. mixing bowl, spoons, spatula
6. plastic baby
7. tape player and Mardi Gras parade music
8. margarine for greasing bowl
9. towel (to cover bowl of dough)
10. 1/4 cup margarine
11. 1/2 cup sugar
12. 4 teaspoons dry yeast
13. 1 egg
14. cookie sheet
15. colored sugar
16. books, posters, pictures, video (if available) about Mardi Gras in New Orleans

Objectives:

As a result of this activity, the learner will:
- explore traditions of the Louisiana Mardi Gras.
- make and enjoy a delicious King cake.
- experience some of the culture of Louisiana.

Introduction:

1. Use books, posters, pictures, and video to explore the tradition of Mardi Gras in New Orleans.

     Note: The New Orleans Mardi Gras has its historical roots in Greece, Rome, and the Christian church. The first parade of Mardi Gras floats was held in Mobile, Alabama, and the New Orleans carnival later adopted the parade with floats. Wearing masks began in 1835, and the practice of throwing trinkets from the floats to the revelers along the parade route began in 1871. A King cake is a tasty confectionery delight that has become as much a part of Mardi Gras as the masks and parades of floats. Originating in medieval times, the King cake represented the gift of the Magi to the Christ Child. A tiny, plastic baby is placed in the dough, and the person getting the piece of King cake with the baby must make the next King cake.

2. Emphasize the importance of a King cake in the tradition of Mardi Gras.
3. Tell pupils they are going to make an exact replica of a Mardi Gras King cake.

Major Instructional Sequence:
1. Divide pupils into five cooperative work groups.
2. Instruct groups, and assist where necessary, as follows:
   - Dissolve the yeast in the water.
   - Add milk, sugar, salt, egg, margarine, and half of the flour.
   - Mix until smooth.
   - Add the rest of the flour and knead.
   - Place in a greased bowl and cover with towel (allow to rise).
   - Divide the dough into 3 parts and roll into tubes.
   - Braid the tubes of dough.
   - Form the braids into a wide ring.
   - Sprinkle with Mardi Gras colored sugar (purple, green, yellow).
   - Insert the tiny plastic baby into the dough.
   - Place on a cookie sheet and bake at 350 degrees for 20 minutes (make arrangements to use the cafeteria oven).

Closure or Evaluation
1. Eat and enjoy the King cake while playing Mardi Gras parade music.
2. The person who gets the slice of King cake with the plastic baby must make the next King cake.

Topic: CONSEQUENCES OF HELPING OR HURTING OTHERS

Grade Level: 3-6   **Activity Time:** 1 class period

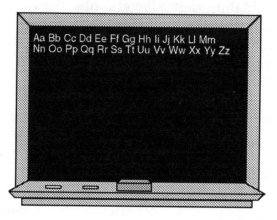

Materials Needed:
1. overhead projector (or chalkboard)
2. collection of children's literature at various reading levels, particularly biographies, fiction, historical fiction, and children's magazines

Objectives:
As a result of this activity, the learner will:
- recognize the impact of one person's behavior upon another person.
- recognize consequences of helping others.
- recognize consequences of hurting others.
- search selected literature to find examples of the consequences of helping others and hurting others.

Introduction:
1. List two columns on the overhead (or chalkboard) with these headings:
   - CONSEQUENCES OF HELPING OTHERS
   - CONSEQUENCES OF HURTING OTHERS
2. Lead pupils in a discussion about the two types of consequences by giving examples and soliciting examples from pupils. Write the examples in the appropriate column.
3. From the stories in the books assembled, show examples of the two types of consequences. (Prepare these ahead of time by placing markers in the books.)

Major Instructional Sequence:
1. Divide the pupils into six cooperative work groups.

2. Leave the two headings on the overhead (or chalkboard) and have pupils print each heading on a separate sheet of paper.
3. Ask each group to find examples from the collection of books and magazine stories to fit under each of the headings. Tell them to find as many examples as possible and write the book name, page number, and paragraph number for each example found on the sheet with that heading.
4. Circulate among the groups, check for understanding, and give assistance when needed.

Closure or Evaluation
1. Take the two headings one at a time and have each group give its examples for that heading. (Encourage groups to involve all members in reading their examples; that is, let everyone have a turn and participate.)
2. Lead pupils to discuss the examples as they are given, judging the appropriateness of each example.
3. Vote on which group had the most appropriate examples for each heading.

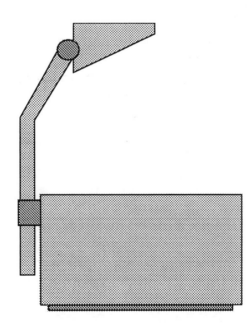

Topic: MAKING AND UNDERSTANDING HIGHWAY SIGNS

Grade Level: 3-6   Activity Time: 1 class period

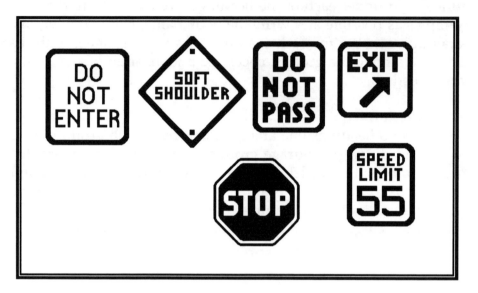

Materials Needed:
1. overhead transparency with some highway signs (use above illustration) (replicas of real highway signs would be excellent, if available)
2. magazines, newspapers, and pamphlets (such as distributed by highway department) with examples of highway signs
3. construction paper
4. marking pens, scissors, crayons
5. tempera paints and brushes

Objectives:
As a result of this activity, the learner will:
- understand the need for highway signs.
- interpret various highway signs.
- create signs that would be appropriate for use on highways.
- make an oral presentation to explain highway signs created.

Introduction:
1. Show pupils transparency of highway signs (or show them replicas of real highway signs, if available).
2. Have someone (a volunteer) come to the overhead, point to a particular highway sign, and explain what it means (class may discuss).
3. Continue in this manner until all sample signs have been discussed.

Major Instructional Sequence:
1. Each pupil explores the available magazines, newspapers, pamphlets, etc., to find examples of other highway signs. (Pupils may also work from their memory of signs on the highway.)
2. Have pupils use the construction paper, scissors, and art supplies to make highway signs that they (1) have found examples of, (2) remember from seeing them on the highway, or (3) create from scratch (must be a reasonable, useful sign).

Closure or Evaluation
1. Pupils show and tell about each of their signs.
2. Hold a vote to see who developed the most unique, useful, new sign.

Topic: MAKING A CLASS BOOK

Grade Level: 3-6   **Activity Time:** 2 days

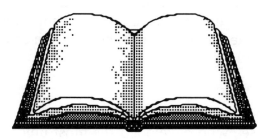

Materials Needed:
1. notebook paper (3-hole punched), pencils
2. tagboard cut to size for front and back cover of book
3. one-inch snap rings (3) to bind book
4. marking pens
5. glue, scissors
6. transparency with a list of possible questions to be answered by each pupil for the class book
7. class book made by a previous class (if possible)

Objectives:
As a result of this activity, the learner will:
- participate in a cooperative class activity to produce a class book.
- write a page about self for class book.
- paste a small snapshot of self on page written about self.
- illustrate a page of book as creatively as desired.

Introduction:
1. Talk about how useful and nice a class book would be for all pupils in the class, and also for parents and other visitors to the classroom.
2. Let pupils examine a class book made by a previous class, if available.
3. Show the transparency of possible questions to be answered by each pupil for the class book (see next page for listing of possible questions). Let the class itself decide which questions (between five and eight) each pupil should answer. Indeed, the class might suggest other questions which are more vital. If so, let them be written on the chalkboard. The class may decide to require answers to five questions and permit each pupil to make up five questions of his/her own or choose among those suggested by the

group.

Major Instructional Sequence:
1. Let children begin work on their written pages. Put the transparency of suggested questions on the overhead and/or have the class's selections and additions listed on the chalkboard.
2. Circulate among pupils, checking for understanding, and giving assistance when needed.
3. Have each pupil paste his/her snapshot on the written page.
4. Assemble copies of pupils' written pages and art pages. Let class select two or three people to design and decorate the tagboard covers and punch holes to match the ones in the notebook paper.
5. Help pupils work cooperatively to number the pages, place them in order, and use the snap rings to bind the class book.

Closure or Evaluation
1. Let each pupil read his/her page and show the accompanying artwork page.
2. Place the book on a stand where it can be easily examined by pupils and visitors.

POSSIBLE QUESTIONS

1. What is your telephone number?
2. In or near what town or city do you live?
3. What is your street address?
4. What is you teacher's name?
5. What is your favorite color?
6. What is your favorite food?
7. When is your birthday?
8. What is your favorite game?
9. Who is your best friend?
10. What TV program do you like best?
11. What shoes do you like best for school?
12. What clothes do you like best for school?
13. What is your "pet peeve"?
14. What other town, state, or country have you visited?
15. What pets have you owned?
16. What is your father's full name and your mother's full name?

Topic: INTERPRETING THE SYMBOLS OF SOCIETY

Grade Level: 3-6   Activity Time: 1 class period

Materials Needed:
1.   copy of the symbols chart above (enlarge copies for pupils) or a transparency of the symbols chart
2.   notebook paper, pencils
3.   drawing paper
4.   coloring pencils, crayons, colored marking pens

Objectives:
As a result of this activity, the learner will:
   •   interpret various symbols widely used in society.
   •   discuss the importance of using symbols.
   •   make copies of the symbols.
   •   create new symbols.

Introduction:
1.   Show the transparency of the chart of symbols (or distribute copies of the symbols chart, one per pupil).
2.   Note that each symbol has a number to identify it, 1 through 13.
3.   Ask who can interpret the meaning of symbol #1. Allow for discussion of the interpretation. Continue in this manner for each of the thirteen symbols. (Use the chart below for reference.)

#1	female restroom
#2	male restroom
#3	restaurant; dining establishment
#4	smoking area; smoking permitted
#5	public telephone available
#6	area accessible to persons in wheelchairs
#7	police station
#8	fuel available
#9	camping area; both tent camping and trailer hook-ups
#10	first aid available
#11	fire extinguisher
#12	hospital nearby; hospital ahead
#13	no smoking area

Major Instructional Sequence:
1.   Using the art materials available, have pupils make replicas of at least five of the symbols on art paper (they may make all thirteen if they like).
2.   Ask the pupils to create at least two new symbols on art paper and write the meanings of the newly created symbols beneath them (one symbol per piece of art paper).

Closure or Evaluation
1.   Let pupils first show the copies of the symbols they made. Vote on who did the best job with each symbol.
2.   Let pupils show and explain their newly created symbols. Vote on (1) who created the most useful new symbols and (2) who created the most eye-appealing new symbols.
3.   Display the symbols around the classroom.

Topic: SPORTS TEAM MAPPING

Grade Level: 3-6   **Activity Time:** 1 class period

Materials Needed:
1. a sports almanac
2. encyclopedias
3. list of various sports teams in the United States, compiled from the sports almanac and duplicated in sufficient quantity for each group to have a copy
4. several paper (or laminated) desk maps of the United States
5. pencils, index cards, colored construction paper, scissors, glue

Objectives:
As a result of this activity, the learner will:
- find specific cities on the U. S. map.
- use encyclopedias to find information about specific cities.
- work cooperatively in groups.
- appreciate differences in culture around the United States.

Introduction:
1. Divide pupils into cooperative groups of four to five per group and give each group a copy of the sports teams list and a U. S. map.
2. Ask each group to find the map location of each sports team and create an emblem from construction paper based on the team's logo (Broncos, Forty Niners, Patriots, Falcons, Cardinals, etc.) and paste the emblem on the map location of the sports team.

Major Instructional Sequence:
1. Have groups use encyclopedias to write five facts about each city on an index card.
2. Paste the index cards next to the emblems on the U. S. map.
3. Each group discusses **if** and **how** the team's logo relates to the location of the team (Denver Broncos--broncos relate to the western United States; New Orleans Saints--famous New Orleans song, "When the Saints Go Marching In").

Closure or Evaluation
1. Each group shows map with logos and shares facts on index cards.
2. Each group tells what they decided about if and how the team's logo relates to the team's location.

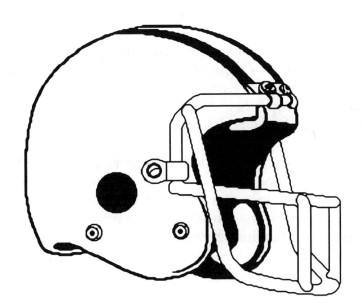

Topic: EVERYDAY PROBLEMS OF THE HANDICAPPED

Grade Level: 4–6   Activity Time: 1 class period

Materials Needed:
    1. blindfolds   3. large belt   5. earplugs
    2. jacket   4. tape   6. wheelchair

Objectives:
As a result of this activity, the learner will:
- experience problems of the handicapped.
- perform tasks with simulated handicapping conditions.

Introduction:
1. Discuss the problems faced by handicapped people. Explain to pupils that activities which they perform every day can be major obstacles for handicapped people. Finally, tell them that they will do some activities which will help them understand the everyday problems of the handicapped.

Major Instructional Sequence:
1. Have each pupil attempt to navigate a course through the classroom blindfolded. Have them try it first without, and then with assistance. This exercise will demonstrate the importance of sight in the simple operation of walking across a room.
2. Have each pupil put in earplugs and attempt a conversation with someone who has no earplugs. This will illustrate the importance of hearing in our everyday world.
3. Have each pupil tape their mouth shut and attempt to relay an oral message to a student who can speak. This will illustrate the importance of speech in our everyday world.
4. Have each pupil use the belt to bind one arm down to their side and attempt to put on and take off the jacket. This will help pupils understand the impact that the loss of a limb can have on common activities.
5. Have each pupil use the wheelchair to navigate a small obstacle course. The course should include ramps, shallow stairs, and tight passages. Also have pupils get into and out of the wheelchair without using their legs.

Closure or Evaluation
1. Discuss any problems that the pupils had as well as ideas and insights they gained through these activities.

Topic: CREATING STORIES FROM PICTURES

Grade Level: 2-6   **Activity Time:** 1 class period

Materials Needed:
1. collection of children's picture books and and well-illustrated children's literature
2. notebook paper, pencils

Objectives:
As a result of this activity, the learner will:
- interpret illustrations and pictures found in children's literature.
- create and write stories about illustrations and pictures.

- develop an increased interest in children's literature.
- develop an increased interest in creative writing

Introduction:
1. Arrange the children's books on a large table and have the pupils gather in a circle around the table.
2. Begin by showing pupils some examples of noteworthy illustrations from the children's literature assembled.
3. Encourage discussion about the various pictures.
4. Tell pupils the old adage that says, "A picture is worth a thousand words."
5. Have some of the pupils describe the pictures, adding any anything the pictures cause them to imagine. (Note that pictures often cause your imagination to go into action.)

Major Instructional Sequence:
1. Tell pupils to browse through the books, looking especially at the illustrations.
2. Pupils select a picture from one of the books, take the book back to their desks, and write a short story about the picture.

Closure or Evaluation
1. Each pupil reads his/her story and shows the illustration that sparked the story.
2. Pupils vote to select the first, second, and third best stories.
3. Pupils rework their stories so they can be displayed on the bulletin board (checking spelling, grammar and usage, and using their best penmanship).

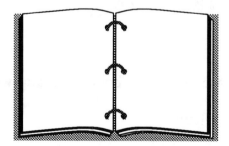

Topic: PICTURING YOURSELF THERE

Grade Level: 3-6   **Activity Time:** 1 class period

Materials Needed:
1.   unlined index cards (4" X 6")
2.   construction paper in assorted colors
3.   crayons, paste, yarn, hole punch (plier type)

Objectives:
    As a result of this activity, the learner will:
        •   draw a picture of self in an imagined setting.
        •   create a photo album of the pictures.
        •   write a caption for the each of the pictures.
        •   bind photo album with yarn.

Introduction:
    1.   Discuss community life in various settings (rural, urban, suburban).
    2.   Discuss different activities which might occur in each setting:
        •   rural = farming, plowing, planting, feeding livestock, building fences, and the like.
        •   urban = city life, riding subway, hailing a taxi, entering a building, walking on a crowded street, and the like.

- suburban = playing golf, mowing the lawn, working in a flower bed, taking out the garbage, washing the car, riding a bicycle along a sidewalk, and the like.
3. Show a photo album (teacher-made) depicting some of the activities that would be found in the above settings.
4. Tell pupils they will construct their own "photo" album, but instead of photos, they will draw pictures of themselves in different settings.

Major Instructional Sequence:
1. On the index cards, have pupils draw and color pictures of themselves in rural, urban, and suburban settings.
2. Pupils will mount the pictures on sheets of construction paper, cut to the size of a large photo album (pages about 12" X 18"), with paste and write a caption beneath each picture.
3. Pupils will assemble the pages of the album into three sections (rural, urban, and suburban), punch holes, and tie the pages together in loose-leaf fashion with the yarn.

Closure or Evaluation
1. Let each pupil show and tell about his/her album, describing the pictures and reading the captions.
2. Have pupils pass the albums around for closer examination.
3. Take a vote to select the three best albums and place them in a prominent exhibit in the classroom.
4. Exhibit the other albums around the room.

Topic: STORIES FROM THE TOWN LIMIT SIGN

Grade Level: 3-6   **Activity Time:** 1 class period

Materials Needed:
1.   notebook paper, pencils
2.   poster board (6 sheets), sticks to mount poster board as town limit sign
     (1 inch X 1/2 inch and about 3 feet long)
3.   encyclopedias, picture dictionaries, atlases, informational books
4.   sample of a town limit sign (made by previous class or teacher)

Objectives:
As a result of this activity, the learner will:
   •   work in a cooperative group to create and produce a town limit sign.
   •   write a short, creative story about a town sparked by the town limit
       sign.
   •   read the story to the class.

Introduction:
1.   Ask if anyone has passed the town or city limit sign for your town. Lead
     discussion about who has seen the sign (or signs in other towns) and what
     kind of information town limit signs contain.
2.   Tell pupils they are going to work in cooperative groups to make a town
     sign for an imaginary town and then create individual stories about the
     newly created town.

Major Instructional Sequence:
1.   Divide the pupils into six cooperative work groups.
2.   Have groups brainstorm, using the available resources, about what information they will include on their town limit sign. (May be entirely realistic or far-fetched and bizarre, even stretching the imagination to the supernatural!)
3.   Groups sketch their ideas on scratch paper and then, after deciding on an idea, work cooperatively with the poster board and art materials to create a town limit sign for their imagined town.
4.   After the signs are made, each individual in the group writes a short, creative story about the town inspired by the group's town limit sign.

Closure or Evaluation
1.   Groups show their signs and give any explanatory information that might seem appropriate.
2.   Each group member reads his/her short story which was inspired by the town limit sign.
3.   Class votes to select (1) the best town limit sign, (2) the best story in each group, and (3) the best story overall.
4.   A classroom display is made of the town limit signs and the stories that go with each sign.

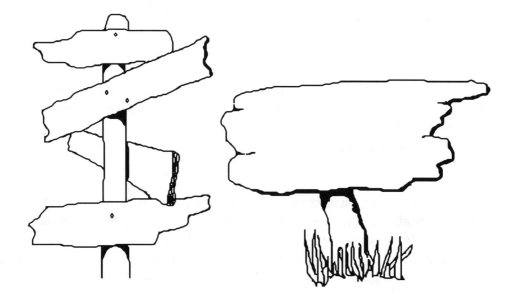

Topic: SYMBOLS WITH MEANING: A COLLAGE

Grade Level: 3-6

Activity Time: 1 class period

Materials Needed:
1. drawing paper
2. pencils, coloring pencils
3. scissors, paste, poster board (6 sheets)
4. transparency of symbols (above, and more if available)

Objectives:

As a result of this activity, the learner will:
- investigate the meanings of symbols used in society.
- create and produce new ideas that can be transmitted with symbols.
- work cooperatively with a group to make a symbol collage.

Introduction:
1. Show the transparency of symbols. Point out the familiar "NO SMOKING" symbol. Ask if anyone has seen that symbol before. Others? Discuss.
2. Point to the other symbols and see if pupils can decide what they might stand for:

- maybe... NO HOUSE SALES HERE!
- maybe... NO MUSIC HERE!
- maybe... NO TREE PLANTING HERE!
- maybe... NO PHOTOGRAPHY HERE!
- maybe... NO PIANO PLAYING AROUND HERE!
- maybe... NO GUITAR PLAYING HERE!
- maybe... NO HOUSES HERE!

3. Tell pupils they will work in cooperative groups to (1) design new symbol ideas like the ones on the transparency, and (2) create a group mural of the new symbols they make.

Major Instructional Sequence:

1. Divide pupils into six cooperative groups. Leave the transparency showing.
2. Have pupils work in their groups to devise as many symbol ideas as they can.
3. After groups have created a good number of symbols on drawing paper, have them cut out the symbols and paste them into a "Symbol Collage" on the poster board provided.
4. Circulate among the groups, check for understanding, and give assistance when needed.

Closure or Evaluation

1. Each group presents its collage of symbols, pointing to each symbol and telling what it means. Groups should plan so that all group members participate in the presentation of the group's symbol collage.
2. Have class vote to select (1) the most ingenious, unique new symbol, and (2) the best collage of symbols.
3. Display the collages in the classroom.

Topic: ESTABLISHING A HOMEWORK HOTLINE

Grade Level: 3-6   **Activity Time:** ongoing

HOMEWORK HOTLINE

Materials Needed:
1. telephone answering machine with "outgoing message only" capacity
2. dedicated phone line to use with the answering machine

Objectives:
As a result of this activity, the learner will:
- work within cooperative groups to establish a homework hotline for their grade.
- connect an answering machine to a telephone line.
- work within cooperative groups to place daily announcements on the homework hotline.

- work within cooperative groups to gather homework assignments from other classrooms in same grade.
- publicize the homework hotline to other pupils.

Introduction:

1. Ask pupils if they have ever called someone and gotten an answering machine. Ask if anyone has an answering machine. Lead discussion of how answering machines work, their value, and the like.
2. Discuss the idea of a homework hotline which would operate with an answering machine. Lead pupils in discussing the necessary steps (permission from principal, getting a dedicated phone line, getting an answering machine, selecting rotating committees to be responsible for placing messages on the hotline, and the like).

Major Instructional Sequence:

1. Divide into five cooperative work groups. Each group will be responsible for placing homework announcements on the hotline each day.
2. Each group selects a chairperson. Chairpersons from each group visit the principal to work out the permissions and acquiring the phone line and answering machine.
3. Each group works to (1) prepare a form on which each teacher can write the homework assignments for his/her room each day, (2) prepare fliers to give pupils that tell about the homework hotline and give the hotline telephone number, (3) select person responsible for getting the homework forms from each teacher, (4) set up a rotating schedule for the group in making the announcements for the hotline, and (5) prepare a parent information sheet about the homework hotline.

Closure or Evaluation

1. Put homework hotline into operation.

ECONOMICS

ACTIVITIES

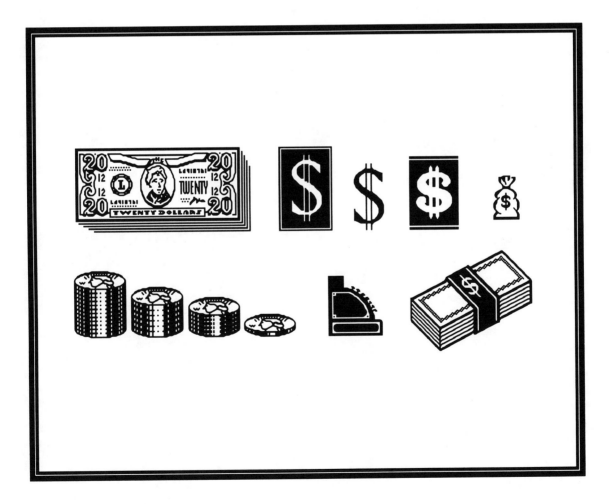

ECONOMICS ACTIVITIES

Introduction[1]

Economics is one of the newer social sciences and studies the production, distribution, exchange, and consumption of goods and services that people need or want. In a real sense, it is the study of how people use a finite number of resources to satisfy an infinite number of wants. Economists study the ways in which individuals use material resources, how *producers* and *consumers* compare, and how *goods* and *services* compare.

Scarcity, specialization, interdependence, market, and public policy were identified by Skeel[2] as important, basic concepts in economics. In that regard,

> *Scarcity* means that a choice must be made in the allocation of material resources — there is not enough of a particular resource, whether money, time, or gas, to put it to all the uses that people want, and they therefore must make choices. *Specialization* refers to making the choice of completing only one type of task. Sandy does only the cooking, while Ross does the cleaning, or the factory worker drills the holes in the steel while another installs the bolts. A *market* means there is need for goods or services that have been produced or provided. *Interdependence* demonstrates that the individual cannot produce all the things needed and is dependent on others for goods and services. *Public policy* is the decision-making process that determines what will or will not be produced (pp. 35-36).

In social studies, economics helps pupils understand how different societies allocate their resources, why different societies use their resources in different ways, and what factors contribute to such decisions. One economics concept that children grasp rather quickly is scarcity because, at some point, they experience not having something they need or want. The concept of scarcity necessitates decision making

---

[1] Adapted from Stockard, J., & Wolfinger, D. (in press). *Social studies for the elementary school child: An interdisciplinary approach.* Needham Heights, MA: Allyn & Bacon.

[2] Skeel, D. (1995). *Elementary social studies: Challenges for tomorrow's world.* New York: Harcourt Brace & Company.

on the part of the child, and this is easy to convert to an understanding of how societies must make decisions based on scarcity, too.

Some ways to pursue economic education include (1) examining ways people depend on one another, (2) comparing work roles, (3) studying different types of advertising, (4) comparing wages, (5) role-playing negotiations, (6) using newspapers, (7) studying the concept of seasonal employment, (8) studying government regulations, (9) familiarizing children with local businesses, (10) studying personal and family budgeting, and (11) participating in simulation games (monopoly, for example).

Topic: DISTINGUISHING BETWEEN WANTS AND NEEDS

Grade Level: 2-6   **Activity Time:** 1 class period

Materials Needed:
1.   magazines, newspapers, advertising brochures
2.   8 sheets of poster board (about 2' X 3')
3.   scissors, paste
4.   marking pens

Objectives:
    As a result of this activity, the learner will:
- distinguish between wants and needs.
- select advertisements depicting wants.
- select advertisements depicting needs.
- make collages of wants and needs advertisements.

Introduction:
1. Make headings for two columns on the chalkboard, one labeled WANTS and one labeled NEEDS.
2. Brainstorm with pupils about the kinds of things which might be placed under WANTS and the kinds of things which might be placed under NEEDS.
    (microwave oven, house, clothing, shoes, pets, eyeglasses, etc.)

Major Instructional Sequence:
1. Divide pupils into four cooperative work groups.
2. Supply each group with two poster boards, magazines, newspapers, and advertising brochures.
3. Ask pupils to label one poster board WANTS and the other poster board NEEDS.
4. Have groups go through the magazines, newspapers, etc., looking for advertisements showing things that could be classified as either WANTS or NEEDS.
5. Pupils are to cut out the pictures, work cooperatively to categorize them according to WANTS or NEEDS, and paste them in a collage on the appropriate poster board.

Closure or Evaluation
1. Groups show their posters and identify the advertisements depicting WANTS and the advertisements depicting NEEDS. Remind groups that all members of the group should participate in the presentation.
2. As groups make their presentations, have rest of class decide whether the advertisements accurately depict either WANTS or NEEDS.
3. Pupils vote on the best WANTS poster and the best NEEDS poster.
4. Display completed WANTS and NEEDS posters around the room.

Topic: DISTINGUISHING BETWEEN GOODS AND SERVICES

Grade Level: 2-6   **Activity Time:** 1 class period

Materials Needed:
1. magazines, newspapers, advertising brochures, yellow pages of phone book
2. 8 sheets of poster board (about 2' X 3')
3. scissors, paste
4. marking pens

Objectives:
As a result of this activity, the learner will:
- distinguish between goods and services.
- select advertisements depicting goods.
- select advertisements depicting services.
- make collages of advertisements of goods and services on poster boards.

Introduction:
1. Make headings for two columns on the chalkboard, one labeled GOODS and one labeled SERVICES.
2. Brainstorm with pupils the kinds of things which might be placed under GOODS and the kinds of things which might be placed under SERVICES. (dry cleaners, blue jeans, toothbrush, waiter, phone company, tires, etc.)

Major Instructional Sequence:
1. Divide pupils into four cooperative work groups.
2. Supply each group with two poster boards, magazines, newspapers, advertising brochures, and yellow pages.
3. Ask pupils to label one poster board GOODS and the other poster board SERVICES.
4. Have groups go through the magazines, newspapers, etc., looking for advertisements showing either goods or services.
5. Pupils are to cut out the pictures, work cooperatively to categorize them according to GOODS or SERVICES, and paste them in a collage on the appropriate poster board.

Closure or Evaluation
1. Groups show their posters and identify the advertisements for GOODS and the advertisements for SERVICES. Remind groups that all members of the group should participate in the identification presentation.
2. As groups make their presentations, have rest of class decide whether the advertisements accurately depict either GOODS or SERVICES.
3. Pupils vote on the best GOODS poster and the best SERVICES poster.
4. Display completed GOODS and SERVICES posters around the room.

Topic: MAKING AN ADVERTISING T-SHIRT

Grade Level: 3-6   **Activity Time:** 1 class period

Materials Needed:
1. white or light colored t-shirts (brought by pupils)
2. t-shirt paints and marking pens
3. carbon paper
4. advertising fliers, newspapers, magazines, periodicals, and the like
5. paper, pencils

Objectives:
As a result of this activity, the learner will:
- design and produce a t-shirt that advertises something.
- recognize the power and influence of advertising.

Introduction:
1. Show samples of t-shirts that advertise a product, a community, a school, a sports team, or the like. Note various styles, illustrations, and wording.
2. Tell pupils that they will design a t-shirt to advertise something real or imaginary.

Major Instructional Sequence:

1. Divide pupils into about five cooperative work groups and let each group explore advertisements in magazines, newspapers, fliers, and the like. Lead pupils in a discussion of the power and influence that advertising has.
2. Ask each pupil to use ideas from the magazines to design a t-shirt to advertise something real or something they make up.
3. Demonstrate the steps:
   - Draw and letter ideas onto a worksheet.
   - Trace the material from the worksheet onto the t-shirt using the carbon paper.
   - Use the t-shirt paints and markers to fill-in, color, and complete the design on the t-shirt.
4. Let t-shirts dry overnight.

Closure or Evaluation

1. Pupils share by showing and telling about their individual t-shirts.
2. Pupils wear their t-shirts for the remainder of the day.

Topic: CHECKING OUT THE JOB MARKET

Grade Level: 3-6   **Activity Time:** 1 class period

Materials Needed:
1. overhead transparency of a segment of the "Help Wanted" section of the classified advertisements in a newspaper
2. several newspaper sections of the classified advertisements
3. poster board (6 sheets, 2' X 3' size)
4. marking pens, scissors

Objectives:
As a result of this activity, the learner will:
- distinguish between different career categories.
- develop an awareness of the marketability of specific job skills.
- determine the comparative dollar value of different types of careers.
- work cooperatively to develop and create a poster of job offerings in a particular career field.

Introduction:
1. Display the transparency of job offerings. Lead pupils in discussing the types of jobs shown, the criteria for applicants, and the salary offered.
2. Have different pupils come to the overhead and point to parts of the transparency to answer specific questions. For example, ask "Who can show the salary offered in the three nursing advertisements?" Continue in this manner until all pupils have an understanding of the nature of job advertisements and the information they contain.

Major Instructional Sequence:
1. Divide pupils into six cooperative work groups and assign each group a career category from the following:

- medical
- business (management)
- business (clerical)
- sales
- service skills (pest control, carpentry, carpet cleaning, and the like)
- technology (computer programmers, analysts, operators, and the like)

2. Have each group search through the classified advertisments and cut out job offerings in their career category and paste them to the group's poster. Circulate among the groups, check for understanding, and provide assistance when needed.
3. Each group presents its poster and discusses the various jobs advertised in the group's career field. Lowest and highest salaries are noted and charted on the chalkboard under the group's career field (charting done by a pupil from the group).
4. After all groups have presented their posters and charted their salary information, the class examines the various career fields and the salaries applicable to each type of job in the career field. Lead the discussion, helping pupils to compare and contrast salaries, training and education required, and the like.

Closure or Evaluation
1. Display job market posters in the classroom.
2. A good follow-up for the future would be a further investigation of the training and educational requirements for various careers.

Topic: DISTINGUISHING HUMAN-MADE AND NATURAL RESOURCES

Grade Level: 3-6   **Activity Time:** 1 class period

Materials Needed:
1. overhead projector
2. transparency (previously made with two column headings: HUMAN-MADE RESOURCES and NATURAL RESOURCES)
3. picture encyclopedias, picture dictionaries
4. pencils, notebook paper

Objectives:
As a result of this activity, the learner will:
- distinguish between human-made and natural resources.
- research encyclopedias and dictionaries to find examples of human-made and natural resources.
- make a list of resources and categorize by HUMAN-MADE RESOURCES or NATURAL RESOURCES.

Introduction:
1. Use the overhead to show the transparency with the two column headings, HUMAN-MADE RESOURCES and NATURAL RESOURCES.
2. Brainstorm with pupils about the kinds of things which might be placed under HUMAN-MADE RESOURCES and the kinds of things which might be placed under NATURAL RESOURCES. (School supplies, books, energy, water, trees, soil, etc.)

Major Instructional Sequence:
1. Have pupils use the dictionaries and encyclopedias and work individually to find examples of HUMAN-MADE RESOURCES and NATURAL RESOURCES.
2. Tell pupils to divide their paper into two columns, one headed HUMAN-MADE RESOURCES and one headed NATURAL RESOURCES and write in appropriate examples they find.
3. Circulate among pupils as they work, check for understanding, and give assistance as needed.

Closure or Evaluation
1. Have pupils read their lists aloud, with the rest of the class judging the appropriateness of the entries and raising their hands if they included the same entry in their list.
2. Have a contest to see who included the most appropriate entries under each category.
3. Display pupils' lists on a bulletin board labeled HUMAN-MADE AND NATURAL RESOURCES.

Topic: OPERATING A RESTAURANT

Grade Level: 3-6   **Activity Time:** 1 class period

Materials Needed:
1. take-out (or regular) menus from various restaurants
2. hand held calculators
3. notebook paper, pencils

Objectives:
As a result of this activity, the learner will:
- work cooperatively to make decisions.
- decide upon menu items for an imaginary restaurant.
- develop and design a menu.
- establish pricing for menu items.

Introduction:
1. Divide class into six cooperative work groups.
2. Give each group a supply of menus from local restaurants.
3. Announce that each group will open a new restaurant.

Major Instructional Sequence:
1. Each group has two tasks:
   - Agree upon a name for the new restaurant.
   - Develop a realistic, attractive menu.
2. Groups work with calculator, menus, and art materials to create their menus.
3. Circulate among groups, check for understanding, and give assistance when needed.

Closure or Evaluation
1. Groups show and tell about menus and restaurant names. Display menus so that pupils can examine each menu closely.
2. Vote on the best menu and restaurant name.
3. (Optional) Plan a field trip to a local restaurant (one decided upon by pupils based on their examination of menus).

Topic: BUYING GROCERIES

Grade Level: 3-6   **Activity Time:** 1 class period

Materials Needed:
1. newspaper advertisements, fliers, advertising inserts, etc., from local grocery stores and supermarkets
2. hand held calculators
3. notebook paper, pencils

Objectives:
As a result of this activity, the learner will:
- compare prices of like items from various grocery stores and super-markets.
- relate the cost of food as one of the major expenditures of a family.
- seek the best quality and most quantity for the price.
- work cooperatively to find competitive grocery prices.

Introduction:
1. Divide class into six cooperative work groups.
2. Give each group a supply of advertising pages from grocery stores.
3. List on the chalkboard suggestions for items to go on the "Class Shopping List."

Major Instructional Sequence:
1. When the class shopping list has been agreed upon, give each group the task of seeking out the best prices and quantities from the advertisements at hand.
2. Be sure that each group has a calculator to work with.
3. Circulate among the groups, check for understanding, and give assistance when it is needed.

Closure or Evaluation
1. Determine which group bought the items on the shopping list with the least expenditure of money.
2. Check item-by-item on the prices so that other groups can validate the claims.
3. Serve refreshments to culminate the activity.

Topic: WORLD PRODUCT TAGS

Grade Level: 3-6   **Activity Time:** 3–5 days

Materials Needed:
1. globe, large world political wall map
2. thumbtacks
3. sheets of duplicating paper, marking pens, scissors

Objectives:
As a result of this activity, the learner will:
- write the names of products used in his/her household on a product tag.
- pin product tags on a world map in the area where the product is made.
- learn where commonly used products are produced.
- develop an understanding and appreciation of the interdependence of states and nations for goods and services.
- become more familiar with world geography.

Introduction:
1. Use the globe and world map to reacquaint pupils with the seven continents and the four oceans of the world. (Use the globe first and then relate to the wall map.)
2. Have some products on hand which were made in various countries (such as Japan, Germany, England, Korea, and the like) and point out the countries as you show the products.
3. Tell pupils that they are going to use the world wall map to show where

various products commonly found in their homes are made.

Major Instructional Sequence:

1. Divide pupils into five cooperative work groups. Each member of a group is to bring in a list of at least five different types of items found in their homes. The list should name or describe the product and tell where it is produced. (Demonstrate to younger pupils how to find such information, e.g., "Made in Japan" on the bottom of a plate.) Possible list examples might include:
   - hair brush..Chicago, Illinois
   - coffee maker...Germany
   - bracelet...India
   - automobile...Japan
   - ironing board cover............................Sri Lanka
   - automobile tires..................................Youngstown, Ohio

2. Each group assembles their lists and cuts sheets of duplicating paper into small tags (about 1" X 3").

3. On the tags, pupils write the names of their products and the places where they are produced.

4. Each group pins its tags to the world map.

5. Groups work cooperatively to present their information to the rest of the class by showing each of their tag locations and describing the products.

Closure or Evaluation

1. Call attention to the world map with all of the tags and lead pupils in discussing questions like the following:
   - Which states and countries have the most tags?
   - Which states and countries are without tags?
   - Do some states/countries seem to specialize in certain types of products?

2. Discuss factors like climate, natural resources, and cultural traits which may influence the production of certain types of products in specific parts of the world.

3. Lead children in a discussion of how our lives are connected to the lives of people living in other states and other countries around the world.

Topic: PLAYING "THE PRICE IS RIGHT"

Grade Level: 3-6   **Activity Time:** 1 class period

Materials Needed:
1. appliance catalogs (Sears, Penneys, K-Mart, Wal-Mart, Circuit City, and the like)
2. newspaper advertisements featuring appliances
3. newspaper advertising inserts and fliers featuring appliances
4. poster board (4 sheets), scissors, paste, marking pens

Objectives:
As a result of this activity, the learner will:
- play a game to guess the price of various appliances.
- develop an awareness of the price range of various appliances.
- develop an awareness of the economic investment a family must make for appliances.
- comparatively price like appliances.

Introduction:
1. Ask pupils if they are familiar with the television game, "The Price is Right." (Discuss and explain: have pupils familiar with the game help explain it to those who are unfamiliar with the game.)

2.   Tell pupils they are going to play a simulation of "The Price is Right" aimed at appliance prices. (Define appliances as refrigerators, stoves, washers, dryers, microwave ovens, and the like.)

Major Instructional Sequence:
1.   Divide the pupils into four groups.
2.   Groups rotate through the following sequence:
   • Three groups guess the price of an appliance (each group making a cooperative guess).
   • One group selects the appliance from one of the advertising brochures, announces what it is, and monitors the price guessing of the other three groups.
   • The group getting closest to the price of the appliance without going over wins the right to rotate to the position of selecting the next appliance for pricing.
3.   After playing the game for awhile, instruct each group to get a supply of advertising brochures, fliers, etc., and compare the prices of similar appliances (brands and models compared should be the same).
4.   Groups prepare a chart showing a cut-out of the appliances compared and the range of prices found for each appliance.

Closure or Evaluation
1.   Groups show and tell about their charts. (Be sure that all pupils in the group participate in the presentation.)
2.   Halt to discuss the findings of each group as they are presented.
3.   Call attention to the range of different prices for like appliances and lead pupils to discuss the reason(s) for the difference in price.

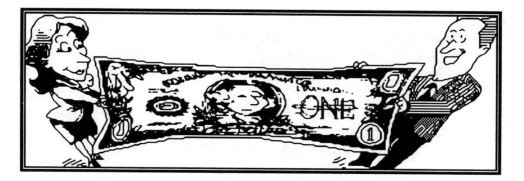

Topic: SUPPLY AND DEMAND

Grade Level: 4-6   **Activity Time:** 1 class period

Materials Needed:
1.   empty box
2.   cardboard coins
3.   pencils that write in green

Objectives:
   As a result of this activity, the learner will:
   - participate in an auction to bid on a limited supply of good grades.
   - define the term "supply and demand" in the context of the auction.
   - generate examples of supply and demand.

Introduction:
1.   Tell pupils to prepare for a quiz on a topic under study.
2.   Walk around the room with a box of cardboard coins, each bearing a specific value. Have each pupil take five or six coins.
3.   Announce that only pupils who write in green will get an "A" on the quiz, but that you happen to have some pencils which write in green.

Major Instructional Sequence:
1.   To teach the class about supply and demand, pull out only five pencils which write in green and offer to rent them to pupils who are willing to

pay for them with the coins.

2. Start the bidding, "Do I hear a dime?" and continue the bidding until you have reached a point where the pencil is overpriced.

3. Continue the auctioning until all five pencils have been rented for exorbitant prices.

4. Now, suddenly pull out 20 more green pencils (or enough for the rest of the pupils), and wait for the reaction!

5. Ask the pupils who rented the overpriced pencils to explain their motivation. Ask if they would have paid the same amount for the pencils if they had known there were enough pencils to go around.

6. Write "Supply and Demand" on the chalkboard (or a chart) and ask pupils to define each term based on their experience at the pencil auction.

7. Mention examples of other items for which demand might exceed supply.

8. Group pupils together in small, cooperative groups of three or four pupils per group and coordinate as each group generates their own examples of items (1) where demand exceeds supply and (2) where supply exceeds demand.

Closure or Evaluation

1. Have groups share their lists of items; in each case, lead discussion of how valid the list items were in the opinions of pupils outside the group.

2. Have pupils record which items were common to all groups.

3. Determine which group compiled the longest list.

Topic: COMPARING ASSEMBLY LINE TO INDIVIDUAL WORKER

Grade Level: 4-6   **Activity Time:** 1 class period

Materials Needed:
1. unshelled pecans (or similar nuts)
2. tools to crack pecan shells (either machine-type or plier-type) and picks
3. empty baby food jars
4. pictures of assembly line workers and individuals at work

Objectives:
As a result of this activity, the learner will:
- determine which method of work is faster, an assembly line or individual workers.
- determine which method of work achieves better quality, an assembly line or individual workers.
- apply knowledge gained from activity to various manufacturing areas.

Introduction:
1. Demonstrate how to crack a pecan, pick out the meat, and place it in the jar.
2. Tell pupils that they will do the same thing, except that some will do it in an assembly line and some will do the entire job alone. Explain that in an assembly line, each person does only part of the job.
3. Show pictures of assembly-line work and individuals who complete an entire job.

Major Instructional Sequence:
1. Divide pupils into four groups and label each group A, B, C, D.
2. Announce that groups A and B will form assembly lines and that persons in groups C and D will work alone.
3. Arrange work in assembly lines so that one person cracks the pecans, one person picks out the meat and lays it on a napkin, and a third person loads the meat into the jars.
4. Each worker in groups C and D will crack the pecans, pick out the meat, and load the jars.
5. Have all work begin when you say start and stop on your signal to halt work. Use a watch and allow groups to work for about ten minutes.

Closure or Evaluation
1. Let pupils examine the results by comparing which method filled the most jars and which method filled the jars with the largest pieces (whole halves) of pecan meat.
2. Lead pupils in analyzing which method was faster and which had better quality control. Discuss various types of manufacturing and whether assembly-line or individual-worker method would be best.

Topic: GLOBAL RESOURCES

Grade Level: 4-6   **Activity Time:** 2 days

Materials Needed:
1. two bags of popcorn (popped)
2. one bag of raisins
3. one bag of M & M candy
4. 100 strips of green paper (IOUs)
5. assorted construction paper
6. glue, scissors, crayons
7. resource maps for Ethiopia, India, Ecuador, and the United States

Objectives:
 As a result of this activity, the learner will:
- read resource maps.
- identify major continents.
- identify the countries of Ethiopia, India, Equador, and the United States.
- produce a correctly constructed flag of a specific country.

Introduction:

1. Review natural resources. Define and list examples on chalkboard.
2. Locate Ethiopia, India, Ecuador, and the United States on a world map.
3. Review using natural resource maps of these four countries.

Major Instructional Sequence:

1. Divide the pupils into four groups, with one group representing Ethiopia, one India, one Ecuador, and one the United States.
2. Distribute construction paper, glue, scissors, resource maps, and green strips.

3. Distribute popcorn, M & Ms, and raisins this way: Ethiopia – 7 of each per pupil; India – 9 of each per pupil; Ecuador – 8 of each per pupil; United States – 28 of each per pupil.
4. Explain that each group is to construct a flag of their country from their materials. During this time, announce periodically, "Time to eat!" This is a signal for everyone to eat one of their resources. (Explain how all countries must consume resources to survive.)
5. While the activity is going on, announce twenty-four times, "Time to eat!" Some of the groups will run out of resources before others. Have pupils discuss how they can use their IOUs to obtain more resources from another group.
6. After forty minutes, three countries should be out of resources and the activity should be brought to closure.

Closure or Evaluation
1. Discuss the methods of getting more resources from other countries.
2. List on the chalkboard reasons countries need to save resources, trade with other countries, and work with others to solve problems.
3. End with a discussion of the difficulties of underdevelolped countries in maintaining resources as opposed to developed countries.

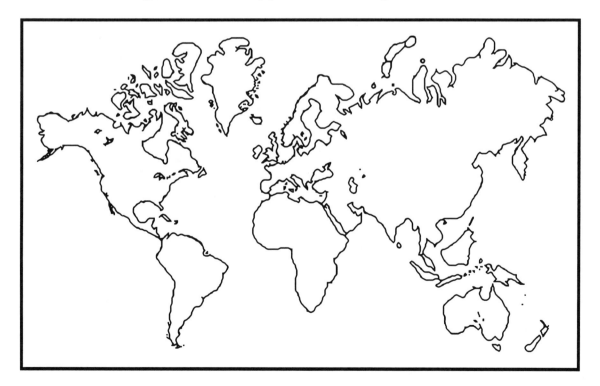

POLITICAL
SCIENCE
ACTIVITIES

POLITICAL SCIENCE ACTIVITIES

Introduction[1]

Political Science is the study of government: the political processes, political behavior, political decision making, and the tasks, processes, and services of government. In essence, political science is the study of power and authority. Perhaps one of the more interesting and intriguing aspects of political science is the study of the ways in which people interact with power and authority. All societies have developed ways of keeping social order. All societies have a structure of power and authority. The governmental enforcers of the rules have great power over individuals in the society.

Central governments expect and demand loyalty when they are threatened by hostile forces. Political socialization is a way of inducting the young into the political life of the society. Basic political orientation is well established in the early years of growing up in a society. Primary grade children can learn that when people live together in groups, they need rules (as an example, give the classroom, the community, the city, and the like). In upper grades, children can explore why nations and governments form alliances. Often, this can be configured with current events studies.

Major concepts to be considered in political science would include political systems, power, authority, political behavior, public policies, and political socialization.

---

[1] Adapted from Stockard, J., & Wolfinger, D. (in press). *Social studies for the elementary school child: An interdisciplinary approach.* Needham Heights, MA: Allyn & Bacon.

Topic: MAKING A FLAG CAKE

Grade Level: K-1   **Activity Time:** 1 class period

United States

Materials Needed:
1. U. S. flag
2. pictures and picture books of the U. S. flag
3. white cakes previously baked in a 13" X 9" pan (5 needed; parents could bake and bring)
4. bowls of sliced strawberries and blueberries
5. Cool Whip
6. a cake knife, plastic forks, plastic knives, paper plates, napkins

Objectives:
As a result of this activity, the learner will:
- decorate a flat cake to resemble the United States flag.
- know that stars stand for states in the United States.
- know that stripes stand for the first thirteen colonies established in the United States.

Introduction:
1. Show the flag of the United States. Let various pupils come up and touch the stars as you explain that there is a star for each of the fifty states.
2. Let various pupils come up and touch the stripes as you explain that the thirteen stripes represent the first thirteen colonies established in America.
3. Arrange flag pictures and picture books with the U. S. flag on a table and let pupils examine.
4. Tell pupils they will decorate cakes to look like the flag.

Major Instructional Sequence:
1. Divide pupils into five work groups, each one headed by a parent volunteer.
2. Have the five cakes and materials located on different work tables around the room.
3. Demonstrate how to ice a cake with Cool Whip. Let pupils ice their cakes.
4. Demonstrate how to place the blueberries for the blue background, leaving spaces of white to represent the stars on the flag. Have pupils place the blueberries.
5. Demonstrate how to place the strawberries to represent the red stripes on the flag. Have pupils place the strawberries.

Closure or Evaluation
1. Let everyone walk around and view all five of the cakes.
2. Take Polaroid (or regular) photographs of each group with its cake.
3. Eat the cakes.
4. Clean up.

Topic: DRAWING THE U. S. CAPITOL BUILDING

Grade Level: 2-4   **Activity Time:** 1 class period

U. S. Capitol Building

Materials Needed:
1.   drawing paper, pencils, coloring pencils
2.   half sheets of poster board (six half poster boards needed)
3.   pictures, slides, filmstrips, of U. S. Capitol Building
4.   picture books, informational books, picture dictionaries, pictured encyclopedias, and other appropriate reference materials

Objectives:
As a result of this activity, the learner will:
- make an individual drawing of the U. S. Capitol Building.
- work in a cooperative group to make a large drawing of the U. S. Capitol Building.
- show drawings and tell something about the U. S. Capitol.

Introduction:
1.   Show pictures, slides, filmstrips, etc., of the U. S. Capitol Building.
2.   Tell pupils that this is the building in which the U. S. Congress meets.
3.   Tell pupils that there are two types of congressmen who meet in the Capitol: (1) Senators, and (2) Representatives.
4.   Tell pupils that sometimes the President of the United States speaks to the members of Congress at the Capitol.

5.   Tell pupils they will (1) make individual drawings of the U. S. Capitol, and (2) work cooperatively in a group to make a large drawing of the U. S. Capitol.

Major Instructional Sequence:
1.   With many pictures of the U. S. Capitol displayed and available, have pupils work on their individual drawings of the Capitol.
2.   Circulate, check for understanding, and assist individual pupils as needed.
3.   After all individual drawings have been completed, divide the pupils into six cooperative work groups to make a large drawing on the half poster board.
4.   Each group examines their individual drawings, decides on how to proceed with the large drawing, and works together to draw a large illustration of the United States Capitol Building. They are to be as creative and colorful as possible. Groups also review reference materials to find facts and information about the Capitol.
5.   Circulate among the cooperative groups, check planning, offer suggestions, and check for understanding. Give assistance when needed.

Closure or Evaluation
1.   Groups show and tell about their drawings of the Capitol. Each group member should participate in telling something about the Capitol.
2.   Vote to select the best large drawing.
3.   Each pupil shows the individual drawing made.
4.   Vote to select the best individual drawing.

Topic: PRACTICING VOTING

Grade Level: 3-6   **Activity Time:** 2-3 days

Materials Needed:
1.   cardboard boxes (about 2 feet square), 4 needed
2.   construction paper, glue
3.   marking pens, watercolor pens, crayons
4.   3" X 5" index cards
5.   picture or transparency of ballot box (may use above illustration)

Objectives:
As a result of this activity, the learner will:
*   use voting to make group decisions.
*   work cooperatively in a group to produce a ballot box.
*   vote on specific issues and committees as a class.

Introduction:
1.   Ask the class how we might decide the membership for committees in the classroom. How might we decide issues? (Lead class to the conclusion that voting is the democratic process used by groups to make such group

decisions. Emphasize that voting is usually done by secret ballot. Talk about local, state, and national elections as examples.)
  2.   Tell the class that they will work in groups to construct ballot boxes for secret ballots, and that they will participate in elections to decide the membership for three class committees.

Major Instructional Sequence:
  1.   Divide the pupils into four cooperative work groups.
  2.   Each group uses the materials available to construct a ballot box. Tell them to use the construction paper and art materials to make the ballot box as colorful and appropriate as possible. Place the boxes in the four corners of the room.
  3.   Tell pupils that they will conduct votes on membership for four committees:
       * class hospitality committee.
       * class cleanup committee.
       * class homework hotline committee.
       * class bulletin board committee.
  4.   Each pupil will vote in the polling place (ballot box) nearest to his/her seat.
  5.   Each of the four groups will take turns administering each of the four elections.
  6.   In each election, the group in charge asks for nominations, writes names on chalkboard, hears a motion to close nominations, passes out index cards for secret voting, has people go to their polling places (where someone from the group is in charge) and deposit their ballots into the ballot box.
  7.   In opening the ballot boxes and counting the vote, a chart like the following one will be helpful to the group in charge for tabulating the votes for each person.

Billy	Sandra	Jessica	Ashley
X	X	X	X
X	X	X	X
X	X	X	X
X	X	X	
X	X		
X	X		
	X		
	X		
	X		
	X		

Closure or Evaluation
1. Groups conducting elections announce results.
2. Newly elected members of each committee have an opportunity to thank the voters.

Topic: UNDERSTANDING THE PLEDGE OF ALLEGIANCE

Grade Level: 3-6   **Activity Time:** 1 class period

Materials Needed:
1.   parchment paper (8 1/2" X 11" sheet for each pupil)
2.   calligraphy pens (1 per pupil)
3.   transparency of "The Pledge of Allegiance" (see next page for model)

Objectives:
As a result of this activity, the learner will:
- gain a deeper understanding of the meaning of the words used in "The Pledge of Allegiance."
- participate in a choral reading of "The Pledge of Allegiance."
- define specific words in used in "The Pledge of Allegiance."
- create a copy of "The Pledge of Allegiance" on parchment paper.

Introduction:
1.   Place the transparency of the pledge on the overhead. Read the pledge so that everyone hears the correct inflections, pauses, and pronunciations. Then have the class read the pledge with you.
2.   Tell the class that the words to the pledge were written by Francis Bellamy of Boston in 1892.
3.   Ask for volunteers to respond to these questions about "The Pledge of Allegiance" (discuss after each response):
- Which word in line one means <u>loyalty</u> and <u>faithfulness</u>? (allegiance)
- Which word in line one means <u>promise, guarantee, vow,</u> or <u>covenant</u>? (pledge)
- Which word in line two means <u>combined into a single entity</u>? (United)

- Which word in line three means <u>a country in which the power lies in a body of citizens who are entitled to vote for officers and representatives responsible to them</u>? (Republic)
- Which word in line four means <u>unable to divide; incapable of being divided</u>? (indivisible)
- Which word in line five means <u>free from restriction or control; freedom and independence</u>? (liberty)
- Which word in line five means <u>fairness</u>? (justice)

Major Instructional Sequence:
1. Divide class into five numbered groups (1, 2, 3, 4, & 5) and assign each group the line in the pledge corresponding to its number.
2. Do choral readings by letting each group read its line in turn.
3. Modify the choral readings by letting each group read the entire pledge in this manner: Group 1 starts, and when they finish line one, Group 2 starts; when Group 2 finishes line one, Group 3 starts; when Group 3 finishes line one, Group 4 starts; when Group 4 finishes line one, Group 5 starts. Do this several times, letting a different group begin first.

Closure or Evaluation
1. Each pupil uses a calligraphy pen and parchment paper to create a copy of the pledge in his/her best calligraphy. Pupils sign names to pledge.
2. Pledges are displayed around the room.

> I pledge allegiance to the flag
>
> of the United States of America
>
> and to the Republic for which it stands,
>
> one Nation, under God, indivisible,
>
> with liberty and justice for all.

Topic: RESOLVING ISSUES BY VOTING

Grade Level: 4-6   **Activity Time:** 1 class period

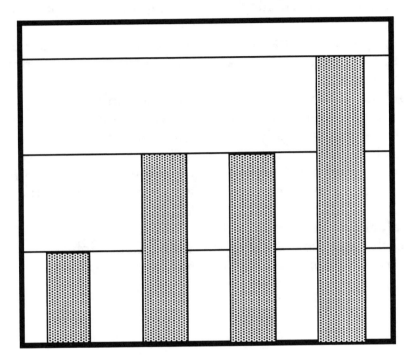

Materials Needed:
   1.   chart paper
   2.   graph paper

Objectives:
   As a result of this activity, the learner will:
   - identify an issue.
   - vote on an issue.
   - chart responses to votes.
   - make a bar graph of results.
   - understand that voting is a way to resolve issues in a democracy.

Introduction:
   1.   Have pupils imagine it is a cold, rainy day. They cannot go outside for recess. They may play a game, instead.
   2.   Allow pupils to stand, suggest a game, and tell why they think their game should be played. Record the game suggestions on chart paper.

Major Instructional Sequence:
1. At issue is what game to play. Explain that different people have different ideas about an issue. Discuss how voting is a good way to resolve issues. Relate that people running for mayor, governor, or president talk about issues when they are seeking votes.
2. Help pupils see voting as a way to resolve all sorts of issues when people live in a democracy. Give (and solicit from pupils) examples from current issues in the news.
3. Allow pupils to vote on the game they would like to play. Pupils should be allowed to vote secretly (heads down, eyes closed).
4. Record results with tally marks beside the name of each game. Show pupils how the total votes are tallied.
5. Model for pupils how to make a bar graph using the data from the vote. Have pupils make their own individual bar graphs on the graph paper.

Closure or Evaluation
1. Let each pupil show and explain his/her bar graph.
2. Display bar graphs by hanging them around the room.

Topic: UNRAVELING A NEWS ARTICLE

Grade Level: 4-6   **Activity Time:** 1 class period

Finding Basic Information in a News Article

Who?	What?	Where?	When?	How?/Why?
A helicopter pilot named Jimmy Gene Tucker, age 60, a paramedic named Richard Thompson, age 35, and a nurse named Trent Robinson, age 27.	A LifeFlight air ambulance helicopter, a Blokow BO-105S operated by Omni Flight air ambulance company of Dallas, Texas, crashed and killed the pilot and the paramedic. The nurse survived the crash, but was seriously injured. The helicopter was going from Tallahassee, Florida, to Perry, Florida, to pick up a patient from a Perry hospital.	A remote logging area west of Perry, Florida, known as Cabbage Pond.	About 11:07 a. m. on November 4th.	The survivor and several deer hunters said that the helicopter was flying at a low level, with high speed, when it struck a 69-kilovolt power line, broke the line, flipped and crashed. There was an extensive postcrash fire. Visual flight rules prevailed at the time of the crash according to the National Transportation Safety Board.

Adapted from Stockard, J., & Wolfinger, D. (in press). *Social studies for the elementary school child: An interdisciplinary approach.* Needham Heights, MA: Allyn & Bacon.

Materials Needed:
1.   clippings of news articles about politics or government
2.   transparency of a typical news article (example follows)
3.   paper, pencils

Objectives:
As a result of this activity, the learner will:
- identify the key facts in a news article.
- recognize the difference between fact and opinion.
- determine a news item's quality by its factual content.

Introduction:
1.   Tell pupils that all good news articles have five essential pieces of information: the Who, the What, the Where, the When, and the How or Why. (See chart above.)

2. Show transparency of news article and lead pupils in finding the five essentials. Let different pupils come up and point to the parts of the news article as the class identifies the essential elements (who, what, where, when, and how or why).
3. Once the five essentials are identified, lead pupils to see that remaining information is (1) background detail or (2) writer's opinion.

A Sample News Article

'Copter hit power line in fatal crash

Beacon Staff

Federal investigators say a helicopter which crashed near Perry earlier this month, killing a Bluewater Bay pilot and a crew member, hit a power line before going down.

The National Transportation Safety Board released a preliminary report yesterday on the crash. Jimmy Gene Tucker, 60, Bluewater Bay, was killed in the Nov. 4 crash of the LifeFlight helicopter he was piloting from Tallahassee to pick up a patient from a Perry hospital. No patients were aboard the air ambulance at the time of the crash, which occurred in a remote logging area west of Perry known as Cabbage Pond.

Also killed in the crash was Richard Thompson, 35, a Tallahassee paramedic. Another crew member, Trent Robinson, 27, a Tallahassee nurse, was seriously injured.

According to the NTSB report, visual flight rules prevailed at the time of the accident, about 11:08 a.m. "The survivor and several deer hunters in the area stated the helicopter was flying at a low level, with high speed, when it struck a 69-kilovolt power line, broke the line, flipped and crashed," the report said. "There was an extensive postcrash fire."

The helicopter was a Blokow BO-105S operated by Omni Flight, an air ambulance company based in Dallas.

Source: *The Bay Beacon,* Niceville, Florida. November 23, 1994, page A-3. Reprinted with permission.

Major Instructional Sequence:
1. Divide pupils into cooperative groups of three to five.
2. Give each group a clipping of a news article.
3. Instruct each group to find the five essential elements (who, what, where, when, and how or why) and write them on a sheet of paper.
4. After the five essential elements are identified, have groups analyze remaining information to see if it is background detail or writer's opinion.

Closure or Evaluation
1. Let each group select a spokesperson (or spokespersons) to share their group's findings with the rest of the class.

Topic: DRAFTING A CLASS CONSTITUTION

Grade Level: 5-6   Activity Time: 1 class period

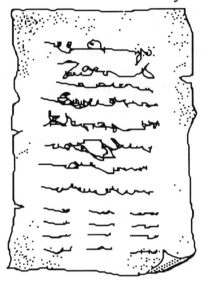

Materials Needed:
1.   parchment paper (8 1/2" X 11" sheet for each pupil)
2.   calligraphy pens (1 per pupil)
3.   copy of United States Constitution

Objectives:
As a result of this activity, the learner will:
- gain a deeper understanding of the United States Constitution.
- work cooperatively to draft a class constitution.
- create a copy of the class constitution on parchment paper.

Introduction:
1.   Read aloud selected parts of the United States Constitution, stopping to discuss the Bill of Rights, amendments, and the like.
2.   Lead pupils in discussion about things they agree and disagree with.
3.   Suggest to pupils that they will work cooperatively to draft a constitution for the class.

Major Instructional Sequence:
1.   Have class select a scribe to write suggestions for the class constitution using the overhead or on the chalkboard.
2.   Divide class into five cooperative groups.
3.   Have each group work cooperatively to draft items for the constitution.

Circulate among groups, assisting and coordinating.
4. Have each group report on its work and let the scribes record the contributions. All groups work under teacher's leadership to edit and finalize the class constitution.
5. Have the class ratify (approve by vote) the class constitution.
6. After the constitution has been ratified, have each pupil make a copy of the constitution on the parchment paper using the calligraphy pens.
7. Arrange for all pupils to sign each constitution.

Closure or Evaluation
1. Display constitutions on classroom bulletin boards and in school exhibit areas.

Topic: A COMMUNITY DEBATE

Grade Level: 5-6   **Activity Time:** 2-3 class periods

Materials Needed:
1. the book, *Old Henry* by Joan W. Blos (William Morrow, 1987)
2. two banks of pupil desks arranged facing each other, about 5 feet apart

Objectives:
As a result of this activity, the learner will:
- appreciate differences among members of a community.
- participate in a point-counterpoint debate.
- collaborate in a cooperative work group.
- understand conflict resolution techniques.

Introduction:
1. Ask pupils to brainstorm with you to answer the question, "What things does a community need?"
2. List ideas on the chalkboard. (The list should include things like people, houses, doctors, hospitals, churches, offices, grocery stores, and the like.)
3. Tell the class you are going to read a book called *Old Henry*, which is about

a man who is different from the other people in his community. (*Old Henry* is the story of a person who would rather spend his time cooking and gardening than keeping his house clean, much to the dismay of his fastidious neighbors. After a dispute with his neighbors, old Henry leaves town only to find out he misses his community, even his nagging neighbors. The book ends with Henry writing a letter to the mayor asking how the dispute can be resolved.)

Major Instructional Sequence:
1. After reading the book aloud to the class, lead pupils in a discussion of the following questions:
   - Why do you think Henry left his home?
   - Should he move back?
   - Will he have to change his lifestyle in order to be accepted by the others?
   - Is that good or bad?
   - Will the townspeople have to compromise?
   - Can this problem be resolved?
2. Divide the class into two groups. One group takes the side of Henry, and the other group takes the side of the townspeople.
3. Give each side an opportunity to brainstorm together about why their side's opinion is valid.
4. Hold a point-counterpoint debate on the merits of each issue. (Different group members can take turns giving the group's points and counterpoints.)

Closure or Evaluation
1. After the debate, each group meets to discuss a compromise of their views.
2. Each group drafts a letter to the mayor outlining the elements of the compromise.

Topic: STATE RATIFICATION TIME-LINE

Grade Level: 5-6   **Activity Time:** 1 class period

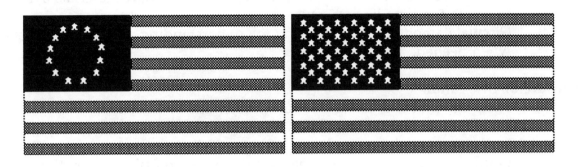

Materials Needed:
1. U. S. flag
2. encyclopedias, picture dictionaries, informational books about the growth and development of the United States from 13 colonies to 50 states
3. long section of butcher paper, about 18 to 20 feet long
4. coloring pencils, marking pens
5. maps showing shapes of states

Objectives:
    As a result of this activity, the learner will:
- develop a time-line showing the ratification of states fourteen through fifty.
- draw shapes of states next to their ratification dates on the time-line.
- illustrate a U. S. flag appropriate for the number of states (1) at the beginning of the time-line, (2) four or five times along the interior of the timeline, and (3) at the end of the timeline.

Introduction:
1. Show pictures of the original U. S. flag showing thirteen stars, of various flags as they appeared in U. S. history, and the latest flag showing fifty stars.
2. Lead pupils in a discussion of how the stars represent the number of states in the United States and that Congress must **ratify** each new state. (Discuss the meaning of **ratify** and lead pupils to suggest some of the following synonyms: approve, endorse, accept, authorize, sanction, legalize, affirm, certify, validate, and the like.)
3. Tell pupils they are going to work together and prepare a time-line showing the dates on which states fourteen through fifty were ratified.

Major Instructional Sequence:
1. Divide pupils into five work groups, each group responsible for a different segment of the time-line.
2. Groups work cooperatively with the resources and art materials available to create the time-line.
3. Circulate among pupils, checking for understanding and giving assistance when needed.

Closure or Evaluation
1. Hang the time-line along one (or more) walls of the room.
2. Invite pupils from other classes to see the time-line and hear explanations by the groups who created each section. (Tell class to plan so that all pupils in a group are able to participate in the group's presentation.)

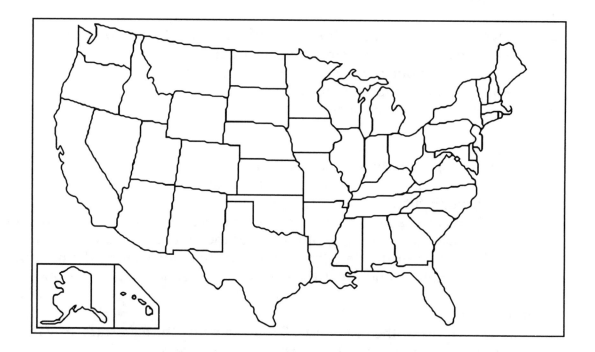

INTER-DISCIPLINARY

ACTIVITIES

INTERDISCIPLINARY ACTIVITIES

Introduction[1]

Dictionary definitions vary somewhat but generally define interdisciplinary education as instruction combining two or more academic disciplines. It is a teaching method that combines subject matter that is usually taught separately, such as science, math, geography, or literature, into an integrated whole. It integrates information from many academic sources and lessens fragmentation. It blurs the lines of distinction between the subject areas.

Interdisciplinary education draws information, ideas, and strategies from several subject areas and disciplines in order to examine a central theme. Thematic units which examine a specific issue, problem, person, event, time period, area of the world, and the like, are inherently interdisciplinary because several subjects and disciplines are combined and blended as the theme is investigated.

> **Ralph Waldo Emerson** wrote,
> To the young mind everything is individual, stands by
> itself. By and by, it finds how to join two things and
> see them in one nature; then three, then three
> thousand... discovering roots running underground
> whereby contrary and remote things cohere and flower
> out from one stem...

Interdisciplinary education is a means by which educators can remove the fences between the subjects and bring them together in an integrated fashion that brings more relevance and meaning to learning. Interdisciplinary education moves children out of today's fragmented curriculum, where each course is taught separately, and focuses attention on how knowledge in one subject area can be used in other subjects and disciplines. It shows relevancy between the subjects, and, indeed, the interdependence between and among subjects and disciplines. Interdisciplinary education is a means of integrating the content of different subjects in a relevant manner which benefits both the learner and the teacher.

Some school subjects, such as social studies and science, may be called interdisciplinary because they integrate other fairly distinct bodies of knowledge. For example, social studies draws on history, geography, political science,

---

[1] Adapted from Stockard, J., & Wolfinger, D. (in press). *Social studies for the elementary school child: An interdisciplinary approach.* Needham Heights, MA: Allyn & Bacon.

economics, anthropology, sociology, and psychology, while science draws on biology, chemistry, physics, geology, and physiology. It is fairly common, for example, to see history, geography, and other social sciences, blended, united, and combined during the teaching of social studies. In like manner, one commonly finds a blending and combining of biology, physics, chemistry, and geology during the teaching of elementary school science. This, however, is integrating instruction within a subject rather than between and among school subjects.

In the larger sense, interdisciplinary education means to integrate instruction between and among school subjects. It spawns the idea of cutting across all subject matter lines, creating a wholly unified program which integrates the various areas of the school curriculum. More and more, elementary schools in the United States are moving into interdisciplinary education. As schools adopt interdisciplinary approaches, social studies often emerges as the umbrella under which subjects that were formerly taught separately are blended.

Social studies, already possessing a broad foundation of academic disciplines and already integrating these disciplines within its own content area, is ideally suited to integrate instruction between and among the school subjects. Social studies is the perfect umbrella for true interdisciplinary education in the elementary school. Integrating traditional content areas under social studies provides an umbrella curriculum which can help pupils extend and refine their knowledge and skills in meaningful, connected ways rather than in fragmented pieces.

Topic: SPATIAL RELATIONSHIPS

Grade Level: K-3   **Activity Time:** 1 class period

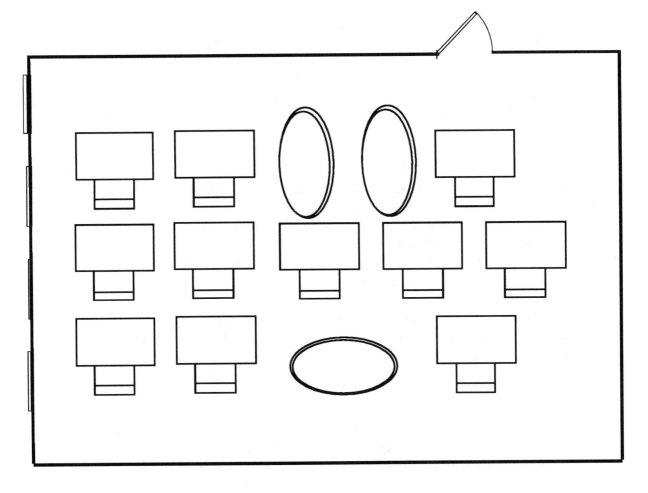

Materials Needed:
1. transparency map of the classroom (prepared by teacher)
2. roll of kite string
3. large, unlined index cards (5" X 7")
4. black marking pen
5. Scotch tape
6. manila drawing paper, pencils, crayons

Objectives:
As a result of this activity, the learner will:
- determine spatial relationships of objects in the classroom.
- describe self in spatial relationship to objects and other people.

- use the string to verify spatial relationships.
- locate objects on a map of the classroom.

Introduction:
1. Have each pupil carefully print his/her name on the index card with the marking pen (teacher prints names for younger children)
2. Tape the identification cards to the top of each pupil's chair.
3. Line pupils along the wall and play a quick game of "Who can go stand behind Jimmy's chair? Pam's chair? Cynthia's chair?" and the like. Continue until all have had at least one opportunity to participate.

Major Instructional Sequence:
1. Determine which chair is farthest from the pencil sharpener, the teacher's desk, the door, the windows, various other pupils' desks, and the like. Do the same, but determine which chair is closest.
2. Each time, verify the distances with the string by having one pupil hold one end of the string on one object and another pupil hold the other end of the string on the other object. Make sure all pupils have an opportunity to hold the string, and make sure that all children understand each verification.
3. Look at the transparency of the classroom map.
4. Point to various items, such as the teacher's desk, desks of various pupils, and the like. Have pupils identify the items by relating them to the real objects in the classroom, such as the pupils' chairs with their names.

Closure or Evaluation
1. Place children in small, cooperative groups of three to four and let them draw a map of the classroom, placing their own desks appropriately.
2. Let groups show and tell about their classroom maps.

Topic: VOCABULARY BINGO

Grade Level: 2-3   **Activity Time:**   1 class period

justice	continent	freedom	latitude	Earth
mountain	seasons	map	globe	lifestyle

Materials Needed:
1. bingo cards (may be made on typewriter paper for easy copying)
2. beans, kernels of corn, buttons, or the like (so that each pupil has 20 pieces)
3. small strips of paper (about 1 inch by 2 inches)
4. pencils and scissors
5. a large box or paper sack
6. a list of vocabulary words that you want to introduce to pupils

Objectives:

As a result of this activity, the learner will:

- play bingo by recognizing vocabulary words.
- increase speaking, listening, reading, and writing vocabularies via the bingo game.

Introduction:

1. Show the pupils a bingo card on the overhead or chalkboard that has vocabulary words in the squares instead of numerals.
2. Demonstrate how a square is covered when its word is called.
3. Tell pupils that they are going to make vocabulary cards and play vocabulary bingo.

Major Instructional Sequence:

1. Divide pupils into cooperative work groups (four or five groups).
2. Make a column on the chalkboard (or overhead) for each group.
3. Write (and pronounce) four or five vocabulary words as you place them under each group's column.
4. Have each group copy each word on a separate strip of paper. (Suggest dividing the work so that each person in the group is responsible for writing one word on a paper strip.)
5. Place all word strips in the box (or sack). Mix thoroughly.
6. Each group works cooperatively to:
   - get a handful (twenty or more) of the strips.
   - write the words in the blanks on their group bingo card (sheet).
7. When groups complete the task of writing words on their group cards, have them return all word strips to the box (or sack).
8. Mix the word strips thoroughly and begin the vocabulary bingo game by calling out definitions for the words as you draw them, one by one, from the box (or sack).
9. Each group, playing one card cooperatively, places beans, kernels of corn, buttons, or the like, on words on their group cards for which definitions are read.
10. Vary by regrouping pupils for additional bingo games.

Closure or Evaluation

1. Call out definitions for the words used in the bingo games and let pupils work independently to write the words they can identify. See which pupils are able to identify the most words correctly.

Topic: DESIGN A STATE LICENSE PLATE

Grade Level: 2-4   **Activity Time:**   1 class period

Materials Needed:
1.   construction paper in a variety of colors.
2.   crayons, pencils, and marking pens.
3.   drawing paper.
4.   several old license plates (from different states, if possible).
5.   references on states, including encyclopedias and trade books.
6.   names of states on strips of paper placed in a paper sack.

Objectives:
As a result of this activity, the learner will:
•   express creativity in designing a state license plate.
•   sift through many details about a particular state.
•   gain knowledge and information about several states.

Introduction:
1.   Show pupils examples of old license plates; discuss how they often have state symbols, such as birds, flowers, trees, or flags.
2.   Tell children they are going to select a state and design a license plate for that state.

Major Instructional Sequence:
1.   Divide pupils into cooperative work groups (four or five groups).
2.   Assemble materials and references at group workstations.
3.   Let children reach into the paper sack and get a strip of paper with a state's name.
4.   Encourage children to be imaginative in combining pictures, numerals, letters, and slogans in making license plates for their states. Give the example of a hula dancer to represent Hawaii (if you use such an example, don't include Hawaii as one of the states that can be chosen from the sack).

Closure or Evaluation
1.   Let children show and describe their individual license plates.
2.   Mount the license plates on a bulletin board, across the top of the chalkboard, or in some other appropriate way.

Topic: GRAPHING WAYS OF GETTING TO SCHOOL

Grade Level: 2-4   **Activity Time:** 1 class period

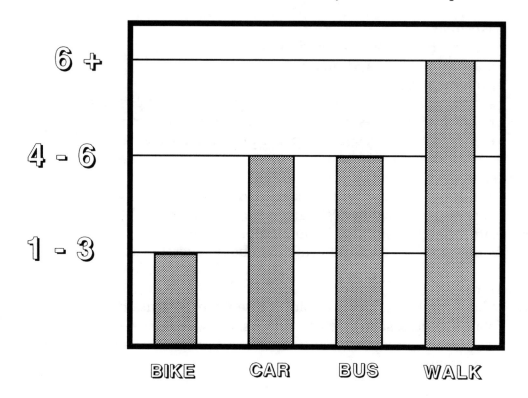

Materials Needed:
1. poster board (5 pieces)
2. marking pens in assorted colors
3. crayons, pencils
4. construction paper, scissors
5. overhead projector
6. transparency of graph on next page

Objectives:
As a result of this activity, the learner will:
- display information in graphic form.
- make a pictograph of the methods of transportation used in getting to and from school.
- explain the information shown on the graph.

Introduction:

1. Use the overhead to show the transparency of the graph.
2. Tell pupils that this graph shows the ways that children in another class get to school.
3. Ask, "Who can tell how many walk to school? Ride the bus? Ride their bicycles? Ride in an automobile?" (Solicit several children to come up to the overhead and explain their answers while pointing to the graph. Discuss the graph in this manner until you are sure all pupils understand what the graph shows.
4. Tell pupils they will work in cooperative groups to make a similar graph of their own class.

Major Instructional Sequence:

1. Divide pupils into five cooperative groups.
2. Make four columns on the chalkboard: BIKE, CAR, BUS, WALK. Ask pupils to raise their hands if they ride their bikes to school (record the number). Do the same for CAR, BUS, and WALK.
3. Ask the groups to make a graph like the one on the overhead to show the information for their class. Tell pupils to make their graphs attractive by drawing and cutting out images from the construction paper to use on the graph.(Circulate, check for understanding, and give assistance where needed.)

Closure or Evaluation

1. Let each group show and tell about its graph. Encourage groups to plan so that everyone in the group has a part in telling about the graph.
2. Display the graphs in the classroom or in an exhibit area of the school.

Topic: MAKING A COLLAGE

Grade Level: 1-6   **Activity Time:** 1 or 2 class periods

Materials Needed:
  1.   old magazines, newspapers, periodicals, catalogs
  2.   scissors, paste or glue
  3.   oak tagboard
  4.   sample collages or pictures of collages

Objectives:
  As a result of this activity, the learner will:
  •   create a collage.
  •   understand that collage comes from the French language and that it means to glue things together to form a picture.
  •   know that a collage can (1) be just a pattern (abstract) or (2) have a subject or theme (depict a picture).

Introduction:
  1.   Divide pupils into four cooperative groups.
  2.   Show examples of collages or pictures of collages. Explain the French origin and meaning of "collage."
  3.   Explain that some collages are just abstract patterns of shapes and colors (demonstrate by example or picture) and some collages have a subject theme like a tree, a landscape, an old barn, etc. (demonstrate by example or picture).
  4.   Explain and demonstrate the steps in making a collage:
      •   deciding what the collage will show
      •   cutting out appropriate pieces from the magazines, newspapers, etc.
      •   gluing the pieces on the tag board in the pattern decided upon

Major Instructional Sequence:
1. Tell pupils that each group will make a collage (either abstract or theme). Note: first and second graders' first experiences should be with abstract patterns.
2. Have groups obtain the necessary materials and plan their collages.
3. Allow work to begin on collages; circulate among groups offering helpful suggestions as appropriate.

Closure or Evaluation
1. Let each group show its collage and explain what it depicts and why they decided on that kind of collage.
2. Display collages in the classroom or in a school exhibit area, such as cafeteria walls.

Topic: MAKING PAPIER-MACHÉ MOONS

Grade Level: 3–6   **Activity Time:**   2 or 3 days

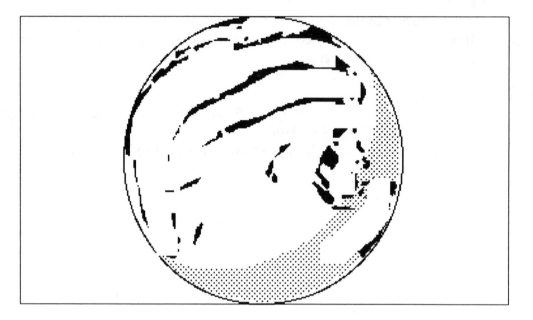

Materials Needed:
1.   strips of newsprint and/or butcher paper measuring about 10" X 2"
2.   liquid starch
3.   tempera paints in assorted colors (especially gray, black, and white) and brushes
4.   balloons (durable and spherical, such as "punch-ball" type; 12 to 16 inches in diameter when inflated)
5.   binoculars and/or telescope
6.   moon maps; photos (available from Hansen Planetarium (800) 321-2369, or NASA)

Objectives:
As a result of this activity, the learner will:
- produce a papier-maché moon.
- paint the moon to indicate mountains, seas, craters, riverlike riles.
- (optional) use moon photos to label some features.

Introduction:
1.   Show and discuss photographs and maps of the moon.
2.   Call attention to its shape: not round like a penny or nickel, but shaped like a ball (spherical).

3. Have pupils go outside on a night when the moon is full and look at the moon through binoculars or telescope (do this as a group if possible, otherwise individually).
4. Show a model of a papier-maché moon (made earlier by teacher or previous class).
5. Tell pupils they will begin an activity to make their own papier-maché moons.

Major Instructional Sequence:
1. Have pupils inflate balloons (younger children may need assistance).
2. Assemble paper strips and containers of liquid starch at work areas.
3. Demonstrate how to dip paper strips in starch and lay in layers on balloon.
4. After pupils have covered balloons with several layers, let dry overnight.
5. Assemble tempera paints at work areas.
6. Have pupils paint their hardened papier-maché spheres to look like the moon (have photos of moon in view).

Closure or Evaluation
1. Let pupils show and tell about their individual papier-maché moons.
2. Have pupils display their moons by hanging by a string from the ceiling, or the like.

Topic: GATHERING NEWS

Grade Level: 3-6   **Activity Time:** 2 days

Materials Needed:
1. a variety of newspapers and news magazines
2. scissors, paper, pencils
3. poster board (3 sheets; 2' X 3')
4. marking pens
5. handout of Ideas for Gathering News

Objectives:
As a result of this activity, the learner will:
- select news items in a topical manner.
- create a poster of specific news items.

Introduction:
1. Divide pupils into three cooperative work groups.
2. Give each group a copy of the Ideas for Gathering News chart (below).
3. Assign each group one of the columns of ideas.

Ideas for Gathering News

Good news	Bad news	City news
County news	State news	Regional news
U. S. news	North American news	South American news
European news	Asian news	African news
Australian news	Specific country news	Aerospace news
Telecommunications news	Entertainment news	Environmental news
Health care news	Education news	Transportation news
Waste disposal news	Housing news	Important people news
Important places news	Important events news	Agricultural news
Governmental news	Endangered species news	Political news

Major Instructional Sequence:
1. Have each group cooperate in finding news articles about the topics in the group's assigned list.

2. When an article is found, all group members must agree on its relevance to the topic; then it is cut out and pasted to the bulletin board next to the topic it addresses.
3. Circulate among groups, checking for understanding, and providing assistance when needed.

Closure or Evaluation

1. Groups show and tell about their posters. Each group member should participate in the group's presentation. Afterwards, hang posters in room.

Topic: CHANGES IN THE ENVIRONMENT

Grade Level: 3-6   Activity Time: 1 class period

Pollution	Weather	Time	Human Alteration

Materials Needed:
1. magazines, newspapers
2. overhead projector
3. pre-made transparency with four columns:
    - Pollution
    - Weather
    - Time
    - Human Alteration
4. large posters of environmental scenes or transparencies of environmental scenes (clearings in forests, highways, polluted ponds, flooded regions, houses or buildings crumbling with age, and the like)
5. poster board (about 2′ X 3′), scissors, paste

Objectives:
As a result of this activity, the learner will:
- identify changes in the environment.
- assign environmental changes to pollution, weather, time, or human alteration.

Introduction:
1. Show and lead a discussion about what is shown on the various environmental posters or transparencies. Discuss what they depict.
2. Display the transparency with the four categories: pollution, weather, time, human alteration.
3. Have pupils examine the environmental pictures relative to the four categories.

4. Have pupils identify which environmental changes apply to which pictures.

Major Instructional Sequence:
1. Divide pupils into six cooperative work groups.
2. Supply each group with an assortment of magazines and newspapers.
3. Ask pupils to go through the magazines and newspapers looking for pictures showing the environment.
4. Pupils are to cut out the pictures, work cooperatively to categorize them according to pollution, weather, time, or human alteration, and paste them in the appropriate column on the poster board.

Closure or Evaluation
1. Groups show and explain their posters. Remind groups that all members of the group should participate in the explanation of the group's work.
2. As groups make their presentations, lead rest of class in discussing how appropriately the cut-out pictures were categorized.
3. Display completed environmental posters around the room.

Topic: GRAPHING EYE COLOR

Grade Level: 3-6   **Activity Time:** 1 class period

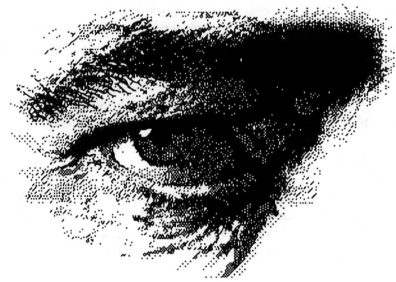

Materials Needed:
1.   graphing paper, pencils, paper
2.   poster board (6 sheets)
3.   marking pens, water color pens
4.   transparency of sample graph (on next page)

Objectives:
As a result of this activity, the learner will:
- survey the eye colors of pupils in the class.
- make a graph to indicate the findings in the eye-color survey.
- understand that humans differ in some ways, such as eye color.

Introduction:
1.   Show the sample graph on the overhead projector.
2.   Tell pupils they will work in groups to (1) survey the eye color in the class, (2) tabulate the results on paper, and (3) make a graph of the results.

Major Instructional Sequence:
1.   Divide the pupils into six cooperative work groups.
2.   Each group makes plans to:
- survey the eye colors in the class by observing each pupil and marking the color on a chart like the one below.

Blue Eyes	Brown Eyes	Green Eyes	Other
x	x	x	x
x	x	x	x
x	x	x	x
x	x	x	
x	x		
x	x		
	x		
	x		
	x		
	x		

- use the information on the chart to make small graph samples on the graph paper.
- work cooperatively to create a large graph of the findings on the poster.

Closure or Evaluation

1. Groups show and explain their large graphs. Groups should plan for all group members to participate in the presentation.
2. Class votes to select the best (1) graph and (2) the best presentation.

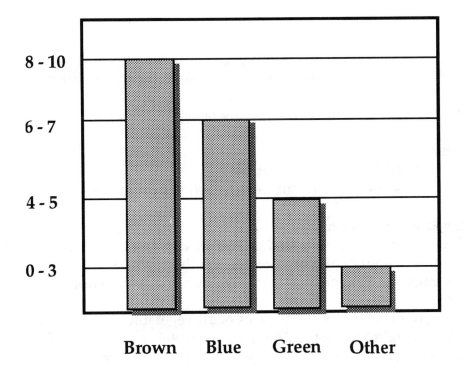

Topic: VEGETABLE IDENTIFICATION BY TASTE

Grade Level: 3-6   **Activity Time:**   1 class period

Materials Needed:
1. a wide assortment of vegetables, such as carrots, beets, radishes, mushrooms, broccoli, lettuce, spinach, cauliflower and the like
2. several serving trays
3. napkins

Objectives:
As a result of this activity, the learner will:
*   recognize a vegetable as a plant cultivated for an edible part, such as the root of the beet, the leaf of spinach, or the flower buds of broccoli or cauliflower.
*   identify various vegetables by taste.

Introduction:
1. Show and identify each vegetable.
2. Let pupils assist you in cutting up each vegetable into small pieces.

Major Instructional Sequence:
1. Place the pieces of each kind of vegetable on a different serving tray. Label the tray with the kind of vegetable on the tray.
2. Let each child experience touching, smelling, and eating a vegetable piece from each tray.
3. Bring out a new tray with pieces of all vegetables on the tray.
4. While blindfolded, let children eat a vegetable piece, and if they can identify it, eat another, and continue in this fashion.

5. Allow all children the opportunity to participate until they can achieve success.

Closure or Evaluation
1. Lead children in a discussion of how the various vegetables taste. Let them describe the taste of their favorite vegetable, their least favorite, and the like.
2. Give opportunities to write descriptive statements about one or more vegetables, such as how they look, taste, and feel.
3. Give opportunities for artwork where pupils may draw vegetables, vegetable gardens, and the like.

Topic: NEIGHBORHOOD LEAF SURVEY

Grade Level: 3-6   **Activity Time:** 3–4 days

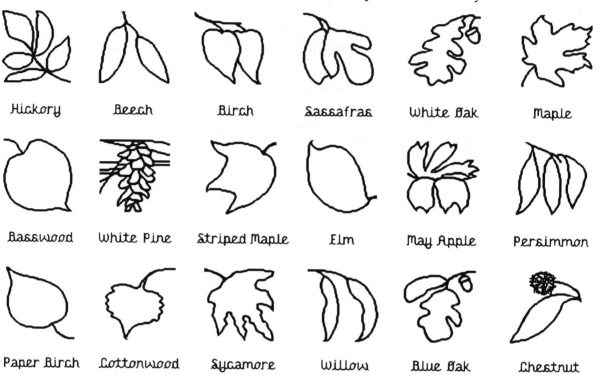

Hickory	Beech	Birch	Sassafras	White Oak	Maple
Basswood	White Pine	Striped Maple	Elm	May Apple	Persimmon
Paper Birch	Cottonwood	Sycamore	Willow	Blue Oak	Chestnut

Materials Needed:
1. clipboards, paper, pencils
2. several paper grocery sacks
3. leaf identification chart (above; augment for local area if necessary)
4. poster board (6 sheets)
5. coloring pencils, marking pens, water color pens
6. outline map of United States (next page)

Objectives:
As a result of this activity, the learner will:
- identify leaf types in the neighborhood.
- work cooperatively to make a poster of the leaves.
- do research on the types of trees from which the leaves came.
- work cooperatively to map the areas where such trees grow.

Introduction:
1. Give each pupil a leaf identification chart.
2. Tell pupils they will make a walking tour of the neighborhood, use their

clipboard and identification chart to identify leaves on trees that they see, and collect samples of leaves to use in making a poster of leaf types.

Major Instructional Sequence:
1. Divide the pupils into six cooperative work groups.
2. Instruct each group to select a "scribe" to carry the leaf identification chart and make any notes they need while they are on the walking tour.
3. Walk carefully along several adjacent streets, carefully observing and recording leaf types.
4. Collect samples of leaves for use in making the poster.
5. Back in the classroom, arrange the leaves on the poster board, glue them in place, and write the types of trees from which they came beneath them.

Closure or Evaluation
1. Groups work cooperatively with the reference materials to research information on the various tree types found. Identify where such trees grow in the United States.
2. Each group uses coloring pencils, watercolor pens, etc., to mark an outline map of the United States showing the growing areas of the tree types found.
3. Each group shows and tells about its map, using the big classroom wall map to make explanations. Groups should plan so that all group members participate in the presentation.
4. Display the maps on a bulletin board.

Topic: DEVELOPING GRAPHIC ORGANIZERS FOR COUNTRIES

Grade Level: 3-6   Activity Time: 2 days

Materials Needed:
1. transparency of the graphic organizer for Egypt (see page 7.26)
2. pencils, drawing paper
3. resource books, including encyclopedias, atlases, informational trade books that contain information about countries of the world
4. political world map and (if possible) political maps of individual continents

Objectives:
As a result of this activity, the learner will:
- develop the ability to interpret and display information in graphic form.
- work in a cooperative group to develop a graphic organizer for a specific country.
- work cooperatively to select a country as a major topic and to select the sub-topics of information to be included about the country chosen.
- make an oral presentation (as part of a group) explaining the graphic organizer developed by the group for a specific country.

Introduction:
1. On the world map, point out the seven continents, noting that there are no countries in Antarctica and only one in Australia (the country of Australia).
2. Point out that Egypt is one of the countries located in Africa.
3. Display the transparency of the sample graphic organizer which depicts Egypt.
4. Point out that the central theme of the graphic organizer is Egypt and that the subtopics radiate out like spokes and that each subtopic has its own group of subtopics. (Let various pupils come to the overhead and point out answers to questions which can be found on the graphic organizer, such as:

- What religions are found in Egypt?
- How many people live in Egypt?
- Name Egypt's capital and major sea port.
- Name some of the products of Egypt.

Major Instructional Sequence:

1. Divide pupils into six cooperative groups and assign each group one of the following continents: North America, South America, Europe, Africa, Asia, and Australia. (Leave the transparency displayed throughout the activity.)

2. Tell each group to select a country from their continent and work together with the resource books available to find information and develop a graphic organizer for their country. (Circulate among groups, checking for understanding, and giving assistance when needed.)

Closure or Evaluation

1. Let groups show and tell about their graphic organizers. Have groups divide the presentation so that each group member participates.

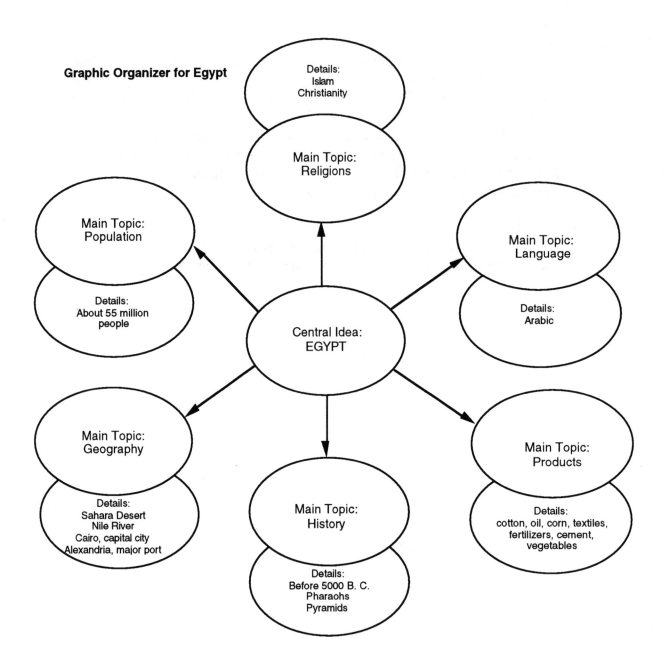

Graphic Organizer for Egypt

Topic: USING COMICS FROM THE NEWSPAPER

Grade Level: 3-6   **Activity Time:** 1 class period

Materials Needed:
1.   several sections of newspapers with comics
2.   scissors, paste or Scotch tape
3.   notebook paper, pencils
4.   overhead transparency of a comic strip (previously prepared)

Objectives:
    As a result of this activity, the learner will:
- convert a graphic sequence of events (comics) into a written description or story.
- select the appropriate graphic series of events (comics) based on a written description or story.
- convert a graphic sequence of events (comics) into an oral presentation.

Introduction:
1.   Display the transparency of the comic strip on the overhead. Lead a discussion on each panel of the comic strip.
2.   Turn off the overhead and ask if someone can tell about the comic strip. Allow several people to give their oral interpretations.

3. Display the transparency again and ask that everyone use words only and write a description of what the comic strip shows. (Circulate, check for understanding, and give assistance when needed.)
4. Let various volunteers read their written descriptions of the comic strip.

Major Instructional Sequence:
1. Ask children to get a section of newspaper with comic strips, select a particular strip, and paste the strip on a sheet of paper.
2. On a separate sheet of paper, have pupils write the story or description of their comic strip.
3. Tape the sheets of paper with the affixed comic strips to the front chalk board so that everyone can see. Use a marking pen to number the sheets in sequential order (1, 2, 3, 4, ...).
4. Have pupils read their written descriptions and let class decide which comic strip each written description is about.

Closure or Evaluation
1. Let class vote to select the best written descriptions of comic strips.
2. Let various children remove one of the comic strips attached to the chalkboard, hold it up, and give an oral description of the material depicted by the comic strip.

Topic: ENCYCLOPEDIA QUESTIONS OF THE WEEK

Grade Level: 3-6   **Activity Time:** ongoing

Materials Needed:
1.   3" X 5" index cards
2.   paper, pencils
3.   children's encyclopedias

Objectives:
As a result of this activity, the learner will:
- participate in a cooperative class activity to select appropriate questions which may be answered in an encyclopedia.
- work independently to find answers to appropriate questions which may be answered in an encyclopedia.
- be encouraged to use resources to satisfy curiosity.

Introduction:
1.   Appoint six committees and assign each one a week of responsibility.
2.   On Monday, during their week of responsibility, the committee is responsible for creating the "Encyclopedia Questions of the Week" and placing them on the bulletin board. The questions can be on a single sheet of paper with each question numbered for ease of identification later. (See example on page 7.30)

Major Instructional Sequence:
1.   Pupils are encouraged to use their free time, as when they finish an assignment before others, to see how many of the "Encyclopedia Questions of the Week" they can answer.
2.   Pupils should use the unlined side of an index card to copy a question

from the bulletin board and write the answers they find on the lined side of the index card.

3. Pupils accrue the index cards with questions and answers throughout the week and use them for the closure activity on Friday. (This is an effective and easy way for children to keep up with the encyclopedia work they do for this activity.)

Closure or Evaluation

1. On Friday, at the end of the school week, each question is read and answered by pupils who volunteer. Recognition is given to the pupils who have answered the most questions correctly. (Ideally, the committee responsible for the week conducts this exercise on Friday.)

SAMPLE

"Encyclopedia Questions of the Day"

1. How long is a giraffe's neck?
2. How does Paris wash its streets?
3. What is one sentence Lincoln spoke at Gettysburg?
4. How many elephants would it take to outweigh one blue whale?
5. Who was Father Damien?
6. How high is the Tower of Pisa?
7. How large is a hummingbird?
8. What was one of Socrates' most famous sayings?
9. What is wheat germ?
10. Who was Helen Hull?
11. Was Louis Pasteur a doctor?
12. What is a gyroscope?
13. How far away is the moon?
14. How many voyages did Columbus make to America?
15. Is the story of Washington and the cherry tree true?

Topic: A GAME WITH TOO, TO, TWO

Grade Level: 3-6   **Activity Time:** 1 class period

Too = more than enough Example: The fence is **too** high. **Too** = also Example: Pamela went **too**.	Use **to** like this: I rode **to** town. I want **to** see a movie.	**Two** = 2 (1+ 1) Example: We found **two** snails.

Materials Needed:
1. index cards (3″ X 5″)
2. pencils
3. chalk and chalkboard space for five pupils at a time or an overhead projector

Objectives:
As a result of this activity, the learner will:
- gain an understanding of when to use *too, to,* and *two*.
- participate in a cooperative effort to use *too, to,* and *two* correctly.
- create sentences when given a specific word to use with *too, to,* and *two*.

Introduction:
1. Show pupils the three boxes shown above (either place them on the chalkboard or use an overhead transparency).
2. Go over the examples of how to use *too, to,* and *two*.
3. Solicit other examples from pupils.

Major Instructional Sequence:
1. Divide pupils into five teams. Have each teach choose a team captain.
2. Give each team a list of words (see next page).
3. The captain gives each member of the team one of the words.
4. The pupil writes a sentence on an index card using the word he/she has been given along with either *too, to,* or *two*. (For example, take the word *loudly* for Team 1. The pupil might write, "We sang too loudly.")
5. The captain takes all of the index cards, has everyone on the team help check each one for accuracy, then returns each card (corrected if necessary)

to the pupil who wrote it.

6.   Each team chooses a pupil to write his/her sentence on the chalkboard or on the overhead.
7.   When any pupil writes a sentence with an error, his/her team drops out.
8.   The team that stays in the longest wins the game.

Closure or Evaluation
1.   When several teams have gone through their list of words with no errors, the teacher may dictate sentences of greater difficulty to see which team can win. For example, sentences such as:
   •   I have far too many apples to fit into my basket.
   •   Billy wants to go to town, too.
   •   He came to the play too late to see the two final acts.
   •   Mother said to Ashley, "Were you too late to go with Trey to the store?"

TEAM 1	TEAM 2	TEAM 3	TEAM 4	TEAM 5
loudly	cold	hot	exciting	sneeze
quietly	run	help	wrestle	whistle
stoves	town	movies	camp	swim
marbles	dogs	puppies	the circus	sing
young	heavy	automobiles	carrots	thin
jump	bad	fast	school	books
dark	the beach	slippery	icy	warm

Topic: IMPROVING CONTENT READING SKILLS

Grade Level: 3-6   **Activity Time:** 1 class period

Materials Needed:
1. transparency of the leave-out-the-vowels reading selection (shown on the next page), overhead projector
2. pencils, notebook paper

Objectives:
As a result of this activity, the learner will:
- engage in a reading activity that will improve word perception in content material.
- create leave-out-the-vowels puzzles.
- solve leave-out-the-vowels puzzles.

Introduction:
1. Use the overhead projector to display the transparency of the leave-out-the-vowels puzzle made from the black-line master on the next page.
2. Show pupils that the sounds of the consonants help them decode the words in the puzzle.
3. Let various pupils volunteer to read aloud portions of the selection.

Major Instructional Sequence:
1. Divide pupils into six cooperative work groups.
2. Have each group create a leave-out-the-vowels puzzle (which will be solved by another group). In creating the puzzle, the following guidelines should be followed:
    - The puzzle should have no more than seven sentences.
    - Sentences cannot contain more than twelve words.
    - Sentences cannot contain more than one word with four or more syllables.
3. Once they are completed, have groups exchange their puzzles.
4. Have groups work cooperatively to solve their puzzles by rewriting the selections on notebook paper, inserting the missing vowels.
5. Continue exchanging until each group has worked through all of the puzzles.

Closure or Evaluation
1. Groups display, compare, and discuss their rewritings of the puzzles. Are some more accurate, attractive, and legibly written than others?

Leave-Out-The-Vowels Puzzle[2]

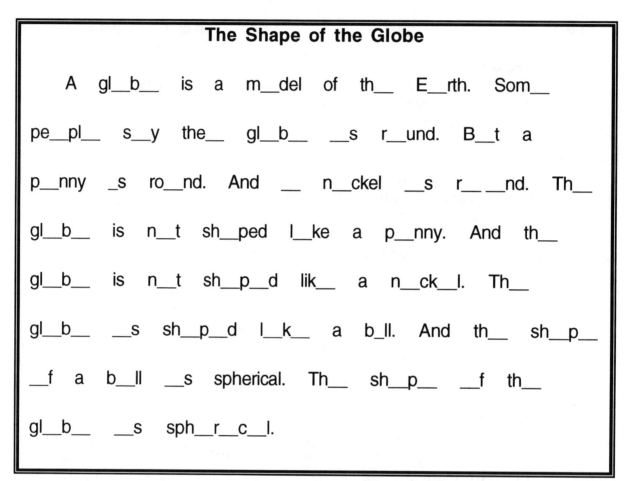

The Shape of the Globe

A gl__b__ is a m__del of th__ E__rth. Som__ pe__pl__ s__y the__ gl__b__ __s r__und. B__t a p__nny __s ro__nd. And __ n__ckel __s r__ __nd. Th__ gl__b__ is n__t sh__ped l__ke a p__nny. And th__ gl__b__ is n__t sh__p__d lik__ a n__ck__l. Th__ gl__b__ __s sh__p__d l__k__ a b__ll. And th__ sh__p__ __f a b__ll __s spherical. Th__ sh__p__ __f th__ gl__b__ __s sph__r__c__l.

Use this completed version to check accuracy:

A globe is a model of the Earth. Some people say the globe is round. But a penny is round. And a nickel is round. The globe is not shaped like a penny. And the globe is not shaped like a nickel. The globe is shaped like a ball. And the shape of a ball is spherical. The shape of the globe is spherical.

---

[2]Adapted from Stockard, J., & Wolfinger, D. (in press). *Social studies for the elementary school child: An interdisciplinary approach.* Needham Heights, MA: Allyn and Bacon.

Topic: RECYCLING PAPER

Grade Level: 4-5   **Activity Time:**   2 days

Materials Needed:
1.   2 1/2 single pages from a newspaper
2.   a whole section of a newspaper
3.   a blender
4.   5 cups of water
5.   a big, square pan (approximately 8" X 14") and at least 3 inches deep
6.   a piece of window screen that fits inside the pan
7.   a measuring cup
8.   a flat piece of wood the size of a newspaper's front page

Objectives:
As a result of this activity, the learner will:
- recycle old paper and other materials to make new paper.
- become aware of the need to save trees and fight the garbage problem by recycling paper.
- better understand the message of conserve and preserve.
- develop habits of conversation.

Introduction:
1.   Put bins around the class to collect waste paper for a week.
2.   Ask pupils to collect used newspapers, and the like, from home.

Major Instructional Sequence:
1.   Tear the two and a half pages of newspaper into tiny pieces.
2.   Drop the pieces of paper into the blender.
3.   Pour five cups of water into the blender.
4.   Cover the blender and switch on for a few seconds until paper is turned to pulp.
5.   Pour about one inch of water into the pan.
6.   Pour the blended paper pulp into a measuring cup.
7.   Put the screen into the pan.
8.   Pour one cup of blended paper pulp over the screen.
9.   Spread the pulp evenly over the screen in the water with your fingers.
10.   Lift the screen and let the water drain.
11.   Open the newspaper section to the middle.
12.   Place the screen with the pulp into the newspaper.
13.   Close the newspaper.

14. Carefully flip over the newspaper section so the screen is on top of the pulp.
15. Place the board on top of the newspaper and press to squeeze out excess water.
16. Open the newspaper and take out the screen.
17. Leave the newspaper open and let the pulp dry for at least twenty-four hours.
18. The next day, check to make sure the pulp paper is dry.
19. If it is dry, carefully peel the recycled paper off the newspaper.

Closure or Evaluation
1. Use the recycled paper to create pictures, projects, artwork, and displays.
2. Display artwork made from recycled paper around the classroom to be a reminder of how recycling can conserve our resources.
3. Try variations by recycling colored construction paper, adding a few drops of food coloring, and/or adding other materials, such as yarn, thread, and the like, to the pulping process.

Topic: TIME ZONES IN THE CONTIGUOUS UNITED STATES

Grade Level: 4-6   **Activity Time:** 1 class period

Materials Needed:
1. a transparency map of the United States with time zone lines (many phone books have maps of time zones from which a transparency can be made)
2. pupil copies of the time zone map
3. sample cardboard clock face with movable hands (previously made)
4. four pieces of cardboard large enough to make clock faces
5. pencils, small strips of poster board (for clock hands), brads, marking pens
6. an atlas

Objectives:
As a result of this activity, the learner will:
- identify the four time zones in the contiguous United States.
- relate time in one zone when time in another zone is known.
- create clock faces to practice time zone skills.

Introduction:
1. Divide pupils into four cooperative groups.
2. Demonstrate four U. S. time zones on overhead using transparency map.
3. Use pre-made clock face to lead pupils in determining time in one time zone when time in another zone is known. Do several examples, letting various pupils come up, point to a zone on the map, and set the clock hands to a time. Have class determine times in other zones.

Major Instructional Sequence:
1. Assign each group a time zone.

2. Distribute materials so that each group can make a clock face similar to the one shown.

3. Have one group set their clock hands to a time and then allow each group to set their clock hands to the time it would be in their time zone. Do this several times, at least until each group has had an opportunity to set the time three or more times.

4. Using an atlas, each group finds at least three major cities in their time zone and writes a different time by each city name. For example, Chicago-3 p.m., Dallas-8 a.m., and Memphis-9 p.m.

5. Have someone from each group write the group's cities and times on the chalkboard.

6. Each group then figures the times in their zone for all cities listed which are outside of their zones.

Closure or Evaluation

1. Groups share results by having spokesperson from group read times for cities. Other groups listen carefully and decide whether the reporting group has done its work correctly.

Topic: MAKING A NEEDLE-CORK COMPASS

Grade Level: 3-6   **Activity Time:** 1 class period

Materials Needed:
1. five or six:
    • bar or horseshoe magnets
    • corks of 1/2 inch or less in diameter
    • sewing needles
    • shallow pans
2. water
3. liquid detergent

Objectives:
As a result of this activity, the learner will:
    • magnetize a sewing needle.
    • make the magnetized needle into a compass.
    • understand that a compass points to the North because of the Earth's magnetic field.

Introduction:
1. Show the pupils a compass and discuss how it always points to the North.
2. Tell pupils they will make their own compasses with a needle and a cork.

Major Instructional Sequence:
1. Divide pupils into cooperative work groups (four or five groups).
2. Assemble materials at group workstations.
3. Have each group insert the needle through the cork and float it in the pan of water.
4. Help pupils discover that the floating cork/needles point in all sorts of directions.
5. Have each group remove the needle from the cork and stroke it (in one direction only) twelve to fifteen times on a bar or horseshoe magnet.
6. Insert needles through corks again and refloat them in the water.
7. Help pupils discover that the floating cork/needles all point in the same direction (toward the North). Compare to the compass.

Closure or Evaluation
1. Lead pupils in a discussion of why the magnetized needles pointed North but the unmagnetized needles did not.

ANNOTATED
BIBLIOGRAPHY
OF
CHILDREN'S BOOKS

Annotated Bibliography of Children's Books for Teaching Social Studies[1]
Key: F = fiction; NF = nonfiction; E = easy book; P = picture book

ANTHROPOLOGY

Ancient Civilizations

Baylor, B. (1972). *When clay sings.* New York: Aladdin. NF, E
    The symbols on Native American pottery fragments are depicted within the social context of the environment of the time. The images are clearly verbalized.

Bryan, A. (1993). *The story of lightning and thunder.* New York: Macmillan. F, E
    A beautifully illustrated folk story based on a southern Nigerian tale sets the origin of the elements in ancient times and climes.

Fleischman, P. (1991). *Time train.* New York: Harper. F, E
    An ordinary class trip takes a turn to prehistoric times, perhaps setting the stage for the beginning of an understanding of evolution, accomplished with just the right touch!

Gerrard, R. (1990). *Mike's mammoth.* New York: Farrar, Strauss & Giroux. F, E
    Again taking a trip to prehistoric times, this book centers on cavemen as well as the age-old adage of working together.

Lewis, R. (1991). *All of you was singing,* New York: Macmillan. F, E
    A colorful rendition of the Aztec myth about how music came to Earth.

San Souci, R. (1987). *The enchanted tapestry.* New York: Dial Books for Young Readers. F
    Catch a ride to the Orient on a magic carpet woven of wonderful tales of that ancient land. Highlighted by wonderful illustrations with the flavor of the East.

Native American

Baylor, B. (1972). *When clay sings.* New York: Aladdin. NF, E
    Native American symbols on pottery fragments are described, illustrated, and placed within the social context of the time. The role of children is stressed.

Cherry, L. (1992). *The river ran wild.* New York: Gulliver Green. NF
    An historical chronicle of the changes in America since the Native American adopted the White Man's ways. Ecological issues are stressed.

Cohlene, T. (1990). *Dancing Drum, a Cherokee legend.* Mahwah, NJ: Watermill Press. F/ NF
    Beginning with the Cherokee legend about the boy who stopped the scorching sun, this book will capture children's interest. Realizing his mistake, he tries to woo Grandmother Sun with special dances, costumes, and songs. The last fifteen pages are an historical account of the Cherokees, complete with a dictionary, a time-line, and pictures.

Cohlene, T. (1990). *Little Firefly, an Algonquin legend.* Mahwah, NJ: Watermill Press. F/NF
    In the spirit of Cinderella, Little Firefly is abused by mean older sisters but is rewarded by marrying "The Invisible One." All of her problems disappear. The last sixteen pages are an

---

[1] Courtesy of Karen Hicks, Elizabeth Partridge, and Susan Wren, Southeastern Louisiana University. Used by permission.

historical account of the Algonquins, complete with a dictionary, a time-line, and pictures.

Cohlene, T. (1990). *Turquoise Boy, a Navajo legend.* Mahwah, NJ: Watermill Press. F/NF
    Turquoise Boy seeks an easier life for his people from the gods. He is rewarded with horses from Mirage Man. The last sixteen pages are an historical account of the Navajos, complete with a dictionary, a time-line, and pictures.

Hinton, L. (1992). *Ishi's tale of lizard.* New York: Farrar, Strauss & Giroux. F,E
    The author chronicles and illustrates an oral tale of the Yahi tribe, a Native American people who lived in northern California thousands of years ago.

Lyon, G. & Catalanotto, P. (1993). *Dreamplace.* New York: Orchard. F, E
    A young visitor wakes up in the midst of a cliff-dweller's community built by the Pueblo people some 800 years ago. This charming story reveals how the Anaszai sang, danced, and prayed.

Martin, B., & Archambault, J. (1985). *Knots on a counting rope.* New York: Henry Holt. F
    NCTE Teacher's Choice Book and School Library Journal Best Book in 1986, this selection is indeed a treasure. A blind Native American child experiences life to the fullest, often through the eyes and words of his grandfather. Love and death are major themes.

Martin, R. (1992). *The rough-face girl.* New York: Scholastic. F
    This is a haunting, bold tale of inner beauty told via a journey to find an unusual Indian "prince."

Reynolds, J. (1993). *Frozen land.* New York: Harcourt Brace. NF
    Glossy colored photographs of the frozen north and its inhabitants beckon the reader into another world - but one so close! The narrative is simple and easy to read. Maps help, too.

San Souci, R. (1978). *The legend of Scarface, a Blackfeet Indian tale.* New York: Doubleday. F
    Scarface seeks permission from the Sun to marry Singing Rains. Returning with rich clothes and smooth skin, they live happily ever after.

ECONOMICS
Wants & Needs
Carle, E. (1987). *The tiny seed.* Satonville, MA: Picture Book Studio. N
    Brilliant collage illustrations take the seed through its life cycle and through the seasons.

Caseley, J. (1990). *Grandpa's garden lunch.* New York: Greenwillow. F
    After a little girl helps her grandfather in the garden, the two enjoy a lunch made from homegrown vegetables.

Florian, D. (1991). *Vegetable garden.* San Diego: Harcourt. N
    Watercolors depict the sun and rain helping to ripen vegetables that a family plants, tends, and harvests.

McCully, E. (1993). *The amazing Felix.* New York: Putnam. F
    Unconditional love and the multiple dimensions of a father-son relationship are presented via a most unique story line, told mainly on an ocean liner on its way to London.

Rankin, L. (1991). *The handmade alphabet.* New York: Scholastic. NF
    A wonderfully illustrated manual alphabet is presented as an introduction to open the world of sign communication to all who see the book.

Viorst, J. (1982). *Alexander, who used to be rich last Sunday.* New York: Atheneum. F
    When wants are greater than income, saving can be difficult, as Alexander quickly finds out.

Williams, V. (1982). *A chair for my mother.* New York: Greenwillow Books. F
    A fire destroys a family's possessions, including an "important" chair. A valuable lesson in economics is learned as the family struggles to cope.

Zimmelman, N. (1992). *How the second grade got $8,205.50 to visit the Statue of Liberty.*
    Morton Grove, IL: Albert Whitman. F
    The "wants" of a class of second graders spur a "need" on the part of their parents to finally contribute to the cause. Along the way, economics are presented, second-grade style, with a surprise foiled bank robbery thrown in.

Money
Berenstain, S. & Berenstain, J. (1983). *The Berenstain Bears' trouble with money.* New York:
    Random House. F
    These incorrigible bears weave a story about money, its meaning, and priorities.

Buehner, C. (1993). *A job for Watilda.* New York: Dial Books. F
    Watilda the witch must get a job to feed and support her forty-one cats. Her stints as a beautician and pizza deliverer can't help but pique a reader's interest.

Ranson, C. & Bond, F. (1993). *The big green pocketbook.* New York: HarperCollins. F
    A fun way to illustrate that although most things cost money, some of life's treasures can be gifts and end up in the big green pocketbook.

Stewart, S. (1991). *The money tree.* New York: Farrar, Strauss, Giroux. F
    This is a delightful tale woven around a tree whose leaves are truly money. The story line and illustrations provide a wonderful tale from which a "value session" may be drawn.

Vaughan, M. & Mullins, P. (1992). *The sea-breeze hotel.* New York: HarperCollins. F
    This is an ingenious tale illustrative of "the American way" of turning a seemingly hopeless economic situation into a profitable one through the use of creativity coupled with work.

GEOGRAPHY

Location
Bates, K. (1993). *America the beautiful.* New York: Altheneum. F, P
    A coast-to-coast journey provides the beautifully illustrated frame through which Katherine Lee Bates reveals America, giving us a varied sense of the diverse beauty of our country.

Brisson, P. (1991). *Magic carpet.* New York: Macmillan. F, E
    A carpet in Aunt Agatha's living room serves as the impetus for a saga which starts in China, leading cross country just for Elizabeth to sit on.

Cobb, V. (1989). *This place is dry.* New York: Walker and Co. F/NF
    Arizonan deserts demand that people adapt to a very different and "dry" way of life. Vividly colored illustrations introduce the reader to spiders and snakes indigenous to the area.

Dorros, A. (1991). *Follow the water from brook to ocean.* New York: HarperTrophy. NF
    This book explains how we get and use water and how it travels across the country in streams, rivers, waterfalls, deltas, canyons, and dams to the ocean. Flooding and ecological issues are also mentioned.

Fleischman, P. (1991). *Time train.* USA: Charlotte Zolotow. NF, E
    An elementary school class takes a field trip across our country and back to the dinosaur era.

Hartman, Gail. (1991). *As the crow flies.* New York: Macmillan. F, E
    This "first book of maps" entices the small adventurer to follow animal characters on a journey from the mountains to the sea and back again.

Holling, H. (1979) *Minn of the Mississippi.* Boston: Houghton Mifflin Co. F/NF
    Follow the travels of Minn, the turtle, from the beginnings of the Mississippi in upstate Minnesota past the "Crescent City," New Orleans, into the Gulf of Mexico. The reader learns the characteristics of each highlighted area through the narrative, which is accompanied with delightful "map-illustrations."

Jonas, A. (1985). *The trek.* New York: Mulberry. F, E
    A very imaginative youngster makes a jungle safari out of traveling around her neighborhood. Geographical places such as the desert, sand dunes, rivers, jungles, and mountains are mentioned.

Jones, R. (1991). *Down at the bottom of the deep dark sea.* New York: Macmillan. F, E
    This ingenious book describes the location of water(s) to entice a fearful child into an exploration of that which frightens him most.

Knight, M. (1992). *Talking walls.* Gardner, ME: Tilbury House. NF
    The young reader journeys around the world via walls that talk of culture, traditions, and history. Accentuated by topical illustrations that enhance the talking walls.

Leigh, N. (1993). *Learning to swim in Swaziland.* New York: Scholastic. NF
    This is a delightful story told by an eight-year-old traveler. Nila begins her tale with her own rendering of the globe and Swaziland's place on it. The story is enhanced by real color photographs, strategically placed amongst Nila's documentary.

Turner, A. (1993). *Apple valley year.* New York: Macmillan. F/NF
    This tale of four seasons can be adapted into most any locale in the United States where the seasons are distinct. The primitive art illustrations lend a different touch. This book could be tied into ecology and/or money themes with a little creativity.

Williams, K. (1991). *When Africa was home*. New York: Orchard Books. F
    "Home" spans two continents for Peter, sweeping the reader up into his jet-setting world. The story lends itself to numerous interpretations of "together" skills, if the teacher so desires.

Ecology

Allen, M. (1991). *Changes*. New York: Macmillan. F, E
    All of nature changes; and these changes are delightfully depicted through sharp-imaged photography of simple settings.

Carlstrom, N. (1993). *How does the wind walk?* New York: Macmillan. F, E
    The reader is taken on a journey through the seasons, instilling in the young reader the innocent purity of our world.

Cherry, L. (1992). *A river ran wild*. New York: Gulliver Green. NF
    This historical chronicle of American changes since the introduction of the White Man stresses environmental and social issues with beautiful text and pictures.

Coats, L. *Alphabet garden*. (1993). New York: Macmillan. F, E
    An alphabetical tour of the family garden shows what delightful enjoyment can be experienced through the simple sights, sounds, and smells so close at hand. A wonderful way to begin teaching youngsters to "smell the roses."

Cowcher, H. (1991). *Tigress*. New York: Farrar, Strauss and Giroux. F, E
    When a tigress and her cubs meet up with a herdsman and his flock, a sanctuary ranger hatches a plan to save the livestock as well as the wildlife. This book is a dramatic example of wildlife conservation at work.

DeSaix, F. (1991). *The girl who danced with dolphins*. New York: Farrar, Strauss and Giroux. F, E
    Adrianne is saved from a shark by a dolphin and takes a dreamy trip into the beauty of the water world, as she becomes a dolphin in her dreams.

Halpern, S. (1991). *My river*. New York: Macmillan. F, E
    The young reader will learn why and how many creatures and people need a river, showing the importance of caring for these delightful waters that belong to all of us.

Ingoglia, G. (1989). *Look inside the Earth*. New York: Grosset and Dunlap. NF
    An artful pop-up book that takes the reader on a journey through the Earth to discover what the Earth gives us and what we need to give back!

Rotner, S. & Kreisler, K. (1993). *Ocean day*. New York: Macmillan. F, E
    The young reader encounters waves and tides, sand dunes and grasses in this delightful photographic essay spiked with a simple, easy-to-read text. A great way to develop a sense of caring for our natural resources.

Pearce, M., ed. (1991). *Plants we eat*. New York: Scholastic. NF/F
    This oversized fact book is punctuated by a cartoon strip on the energy crisis and caricatures pointing out some fun facts. Real-life color photographs add to the pleasure of reading science!

Peet, B. (1970). *The Wump world.* Boston: Houghton Mifflin. F
  A small, clean world, "just perfect" for the Wumps, is unceremoniously invaded by iron and steel monsters, puffing smoke and spitting fire, causing the Wumps to become victims of events beyond their control.

Shelby, A. *What to do about pollution.* (1993). New York: Orchard Books. F, E
  Dramatically colored scenarios bring home the fact that love can be the answer to our worldly problems of pollution, hunger, sickness, sadness, and loneliness.

Siebert, D. *Sierra.* (1991). New York: HarperCollins. F, E
  Through a collaboration of poetry and colorful illustrations, the majestic mountains reveal the cycle of life, season after season.

Van Allsburg, C. (1990). *Just a dream.* Boston: Houghton Mifflin. F
  Walter is a true litterbug who is taken on a dream journey into the future one night. When he wakens, he remembers the nightmarish visions from his dream and changes his tune! Wonderfully illustrated.

Wiesner, D. (1992). *June 29, 1999.* New York: Houghton Mifflin. F
  A junior-high science experiment turns into front-page news as gigantic vegetables float to Earth, causing both economic concern and delight. This story adds a twist to the "junk in space" issue.

HISTORY
U. S. History
Anno, M. (1983). *Anno's U.S.A.* New York: Philomel Books. F
  A "traveler" turns back the pages of time, explores the United States from west to east, and ends with a vision of the *Mayflower* and a glimpse of the *Santa Maria* on the horizon. This book offers a unique approach to our country's history.

Axelrod, A. & Phillips, C. (1992). *What every American should know about American history: Two hundred events that shaped the nation.* Holbrook, MA: Bob Adams. NF
  A "must read!" The American Dream is presented from a different perspective in this book.

Bunting, E. (1990). *The wall.* New York: Houghton Mifflin. F/NF
  Told from a child's perspective, the Vietnam Wall's story evokes wonderful emotion in keeping with the meaning of the memorial. The text is enhanced with soft watercolors.

Cherry, L. (1992). *A river ran wild.* New York: Gulliver Green. NF
  This historical novel chronicles the changes in America since the Native American adopted the White Man's ways. Ecological issues such as water pollution are stressed.

Cohlene, T. (1990). *Ka-ha-si and the loon.* Vero Beach, FL: Rourke Corp. F/NF
  Primitive art with splashes of color introduce the reader to the Eskimo through a simply told folk legend. The last few pages give straight facts on this segment of America, complete with glossary, dates, and maps.

Fraser, M. (1993). *Ten mile day and the building of the transcontinental railroad.* New York: Henry Holt. NF
One of America's greatest achievements is authentically presented, yet manages to highlight personal struggles of divergent peoples working together while maintaining a truly historic portrayal. The illustrations add color and information to the work.

Gerrard, R. (1989). *Rosie and the rustlers.* New York: Farrar, Strauss and Girod. F
A cattle rustler, Utah Dan, and Rosie make the Old West come alive.

Gibbons, G. (1993). *Pirates, robbers of the high seas.* Boston: Little, Brown. F/NF
Wonderful illustrations bring the high seas to life, giving the reader a true accounting of the dangers and dramas of pirates, ships, and captains.

Gordon, P. & Snow, R. (1992). *Kids learn America.* Charlotte, VT: Williamson. NF
Readers learn the history of our great country as well as geography as the authors make every region of our country come alive. This book appeals to multiple learning styles and is a "must read" for all students.

Heymsfeld, C. (1992). *Where was George Washington?* Mount Vernon, VA: Mount Vernon Ladies Association. F/NF
The adventures of Liberty, the calico cat, take the reader through pages sparked with bright illustrations, drawing on authentic episodes from Washington's diaries and letters.

Jin, S. (1991). *My first American friend.* Milwaukee: Raintree Publishers. NF
This delightfully illustrated story is TRUE - a tale of a Chinese couple whose devotion to their education brought them to America, where their six-year-old daughter eventually joined them. A creative instructor can weave immigration, illegal/legal alien status and eventual citizenship into the sharing of this tale.

Levinson, R. (1993). *Soon, Annala.* New York: Garden. F, E
A poignant story of "coming to America" is told by a recently immigrated little girl as she anxiously awaits the arrival of her brothers. She seems to burst at the seams with impatience as she cannot wait to share with them the secrets of her new-found country.

Sis, P. (1991). *Follow the dream.* New York: The Trumpet Club. NF
An insightful tale of Columbus's discovery of America told by someone who knows the value of this discovery, as the author grew up behind the Iron Curtain. This book is enhanced by wonderful illustrations, including a surrealistic centerfold world map.

Turner, A. (1992). *Kate's trunk.* New York: Macmillan. F, E
Young readers experience the beginnings of the American Revolution though vivid glimpses of a true incident that happened to one of the author's ancestors.

POLITICAL SCIENCE

Citizenship

Caudill, R. (1966). *Did you carry the flag today, Charley?* New York: Holt, Rinehart and Winston. F
A young Appalachian Mountain boy brimming with energy and curiosity is honored when he

is selected to carry the flag because of his election as "most helpful student."

Jin, S. (1991). *My first American friend.* Milwaukee: Raintree Publishers. NF
    This delightfully illustrated story is TRUE - a tale of a Chinese couple whose devotion to their education brought them to America, where their six-year-old daughter eventually joined them. A creative instructor can weave immigration, illegal/legal alien status and eventual citizenship into the sharing of this tale.

Krasilousky, P. (1960). *Benny's flag.* New York: World Publishing. NF
    This is a true and inspiring story of a young boy who designs the official flag of Alaska.

O'Brien, A. (1993). *Who belongs here?* Gardner, MA: Tilbury House. F
    This book is a "double-dip," as the author weaves two texts throughout the book. Nary's story is that of a Cambodian refugee and orphan coming to America. The author gives factual information on immigration.

O'Connor, K. (1992). *Dan Thuy's new life in America.* Minneapolis: Lerner. F
    The excitement of a new culture combines with a tad of homesickness to make this story interesting. Dan Thuy is a thirteen-year-old Vietnamese refugee who encounters much that is new and exciting as she works to make America her new home.

Westridge Young Writers Workshop (1992). *Kids explore America's Hispanic heritage.*
    Santa Fe, NM: John Muir. NF
Westridge Young Writers Workshop (Unpublished). *Kids explore America's African-American heritage.* Santa Fe, NM: John Muir. NF
    Each of these books beautifully depicts the roots and customs of a different ethnic group in our melting pot of cultures.

U. S. Government
Axelrod, A. & Phillips, C. (1992). *What every American should know about American history.*
    Holbrook, MA: Bob Adams. NF
    A "must read"! The authors give a fresh perspective on the "American Dream," as they share 200 events that have shaped our great nation.

Levy, E. (1987) *If you were there when they signed the Constitution.* New York:
    Scholastic. NF
    A simple history of our Constitution and an explanation of the Bill of Rights. Interspersed with graphics.

Peg, G. (1981). *Alex, the amazing juggler.* New York: Holt, Rinehart and Winston. F
    This extraordinarily insightful book sets the story line in a mythical monarchy. Through the comic-strip antics of a young juggler, a tale with a moral unfolds, making a strong case for democracy!

Pilkey, D. (1987). *World War One.* Kansas City, MO: Landmark Editions. F
    A uniquely illustrated saga promoting, without didactics, the "American Dream" of peace through the use of a thought-provoking parable.

SOCIOLOGY

Family, Friends, and Me

Bergstrom, G. (1990). *Alfie Atkins and his secret friends.* New York: R&S. F, E
   Alfie and his Dad go through the ups and downs of a normal day just a little bit better, thanks to Malcolm, an imaginary friend who reminds Dad to be just a little bit more patient.

Carson, J. (1992). *You hold me and I'll hold you.* New York: Orchard. F, E
   This time, it's not a funeral in the backyard for a beloved pet. This time it is a funeral in the big-people's world. Words and pictures express both worry and comfort with heartfelt simplicity.

Gilson, J. (1992). *You cheat!* New York: Macmillan. F, E
   A lesson in fair play is told delightfully by card-playing fish. Wonderful illustrations enhance the entertainment value of this treasure.

Gliori, D. (1991). *New big sister.* New York: Bradbury. F, E
   A delightfully depicted story for future big sisters and brothers, this true-to-life story tells about all the smiles and the tears leading up to the big event.

Henwood, S. (1991). *The troubled village.* New York: Farrar, Strauss Giroux. F, E
   Very selfish townspeople wake up one day and realize that a bigger-than-life problem can only be solved if they all work together.

Johnson, A. (1989). *Tell me a story.* New York: Orchard. F
   The secure, loving bonds between generations of a family are exemplified through dialogue about fond memories. The oral tradition between grandparent, parent, and child keep the family history alive.

Joyce, W. (1992). *Bentley and egg.* New York: Macmillan. F, E
   This artistically illustrated book is a celebration of new life, friendship, and fatherhood, laced with delightful comedy.

Hoffman, P. (1991). *Meatball.* New York: Harper. F, E
   Getting along in a multicultural daycare setting is brought to life with spirited watercolor illustrations and appropriate action-happenings.

McNulty, F. (1994). *A snake in the house.* New York: Scholastic. F
   This boy's best friend is a slithering, adventurous, garden snake who keeps the entire household squirming. He identifies with the snake's need to be free and at home in the wild.

Spinelli, E. (1993). *Boy, can he dance!* New York: Four Winds Press. F
   A story with a moral which many parents should read. Following in Dad's footsteps is not always the way to go. A wonderful expression of individualization.

Spohn, F. (1991). *Introducing Fanny.* New York: Orchard Books. F
   Personification transforms a pear into a little girl, turning stories of family and friendship into "tart delights."

Yee, P. & Chan, H. (1992). *Roses sing on new snow*. New York: Macmillan. F
   Billed as a "delicious tale," this delightfully illustrated story explores old-world tradition in light of new-world values, highlighting the age-old controversy of male/female work roles.

Zucker, D. (1993). *Uncle Carmello*. New York: Macmillan. F
   This is a heartwarming story which allows culture and tradition to be bridged across generations.

Festivals
Baylor, B. (1986). *I'm in charge of celebrations*. New York: Macmillan. F
   The desert comes alive with colorful illustrations as the narrative weaves a personal celebration of LIFE! This is a "must read" for life's value comparison!

Behrens, J. (1978). *Fiesta! Cinco de Mayo*. Chicago: Children's Press. NF
   Glossy pages with colored photographs invite the reader to take part in a wonderfully exciting Mexican holiday.

Hurd, T. (1984). *Mama don't allow*. Hong Kong: HarperTrophy. F, E
   This Louisiana, Cajun-style festival has an alligator band having the time of their lives, until they discover that the menu for this paddleboat party includes Swamp Band Soup. Songs are included.

Livingston, M. (1991). *Celebrations*. New York: Holiday House. NF
   Simply wonderful illustrations serve as a colorful backdrop for poetry geared to those "special days."

Tompert, A. (1991). *Sabrina, the gypsy dancer*. New York: Macmillan. F/NF
   The magic and color of the gypsy dance come to life in this strikingly illustrated story. This tale can also serve as a didactic on family and tribal relationship.

Wild, M. & Vivas, J. (1991). *Let the celebrations begin!* New York: Orchard Books. F/NF
   A heartwarming story about the first "high holidays" celebrated by the Jewish people in Belsen immediately following the Holocaust.

Wohl, L. (1991). *Matzoh Mouse*. New York: HarperCollins. F/NF
   Wonderfully illustrated, this story line reveals the traditions of Passover while portraying a little girl who is "just a little girl" - any religion, USA!

RESOURCES
AND
ADDRESSES

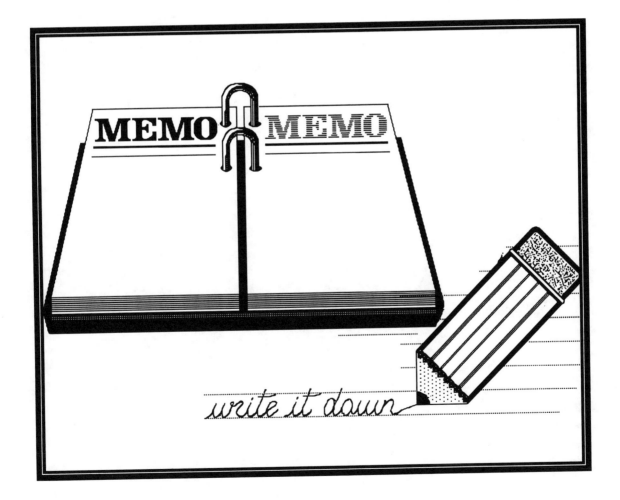

Resources and Addresses for Social Studies Teachers

American Association for the Advancement of
Science
1333 H Street, NW
Washington, DC 20005

American Alliance for Health, Physical
Education, Recreation and Dance
1900 Association Drive
Reston, VA 22091

American Association of School Administrators
1801 N. Moore Street
Arlington, VA 22209-9988

American Counseling Association
5999 Stevenson Avenue
Alexandria, VA 22304

American Council on Education
One Dupont Circle, NW, Suite 800
Washington, DC 20036

Association for Childhood Education
International
11501 Georgia Avenue, Suite 315
Wheaton, MD 20902

Alliance for Curriculum Reform
2000 Clarendon Blvd.
Arlington, VA 22201

American Educational Research Association
1230 17th Street, NW
Washington, DC 20036

American Federation of Teachers
555 New Jersey Ave., NW
Washington, DC 20001

American Library Association
50 East Huron
Chicago, IL 60611

American Montessori Society
150 Fifth Avenue, Suite 203
New York, NY 10011

American School Counselor Association
5999 Stevenson Avenue
Alexandria, VA 22304

Association for Supervision and Curriculum
Development
1250 N. Pitt Street
Alexandria, VA 22314-1453

Council for American Private Education
1726 M Street, NW
Washington, DC 20036

Council for Basic Education
725 15th Street, NW
Washington, DC 20005

Council of Chief State School Officers
One Massachusetts Ave., NW, Suite 700
Washington, DC 20001-1431

Children's Defense Fund
122 C Street, NW
Washington, DC 20001

Council for Exceptional Children
1920 Association Drive
Reston, VA 22091

Council of Educational Facility Planners
International
941 Chatham Lane, Suite 217
Columbus, OH 43221

Character Education Institute
Dimension II Building
8918 Tesoro Drive, Suite 220
San Antonio, TX 78217-6253

Center for Media and Values
1962 S. Shenandoah Street
Los Angeles, CA 90034

Children's Book Council
568 Broadway
New York, NY 10012-3225

Resources and Addresses for Social Studies Teachers

The Council of Great City Schools
1413 K Street, NW, Suite 400
Washington, DC 20005

Department of Defense Dependents Schools
1225 Jefferson Davis Highway
Crystal Gateway #2 - Suite 1500
Arlington, VA 22202

Education Commission of the States
707 17th Street, Suite 2700
Denver, CO 80202-3427

Educational Research Service, Inc.
2000 Clarendon Blvd.
Arlington, VA 22201

Educational Testing Service
Rosedale Road
Princeton, NJ 08541

International Reading Association
P.O. Box 8139
Newark, DE 19714-8139

International Schools Services
P.O. Box 5910
Princeton, NJ 08543

International Technology Education Association
1914 Association Drive
Reston, VA 22091

Literacy Volunteers of America
5795 Widewaters Parkway
Syracuse, NY 13214-1846

Music Educators National Conference
1902 Association Drive
Reston, VA 22091

National Alliance of Black School Educators
2816 Georgia Avenue, NW, Ste. 4
Washington, DC 20001

National Association for Bilingual Education
1220 L Street, NW, Suite 605
Washington, DC 20005-4018

National Association of Biology Teachers
11250 Roger Bacon Drive, Ste. 19
Reston, VA 22091

National Art Education Association
1916 Association Drive
Reston, VA 22091

National Association of Elementary School
Principals
1615 Duke Street
Alexandria, VA 22314-3483

National Association for the Education of Young
Children
1834 Connecticut Avenue, NW
Washington, DC 20009

National Association of Independent Schools
75 Federal Street, 6th Floor
Boston, MA 02110

National Association of Partners in Education
209 Madison Street, Suite 401
Alexandria, VA 22314

National Association of State Boards of
Education
1012 Cameron Street
Alexandria, VA 22314

National Association of State Directors of
Special Education, Inc.
King Street Station I
1800 Diagonal Road, Suite 320
Alexandria, VA 22314

National Association of Secondary School
Principals
1904 Association Drive
Reston, VA 22091

Resources and Addresses for Social Studies Teachers

National Head Start Association
1220 King Street, Suite 200
Alexandria, VA 22314

National Catholic Education Association
Suite 100
1077 30th Street, NW
Washington, DC 20007-38852

National Congress of Parents and Teachers
700 North Rush Street
Chicago, IL 60611-2571

National Council for Geographic Education
16a Leonard Hall
Indiana University of Pennsylvania
Indiana, PA 15705

National Council of Teachers of English
1111 Kenyon Road
Urbana, IL 61801

National Council of Teachers of Mathematics
1906 Association Drive
Reston, VA 22091

National Council for the Social Studies
3501 Newark St., NW
Washington, DC 20016

National Education Association
1201 16th Street, NW
Washington, DC 20036

National Governors Association
444 N. Capitol Street
Washington, DC 20001

National Home Study Council
1601 18th Street, NW
Washington, DC 20009

National Middle School Association
4807 Evanswood Drive
Columbus, OH 43229

National School Boards Association
1680 Duke Street
Alexandria, VA 22314

National Science Resources Center
Smithsonian Institution - National Academy of Sciences
900 Jefferson Drive, SW
Washington, DC 20560

National Study of School Evaluation
5201 Leesburg Pike
Falls Church, VA 22209

National Science Teachers Association
1742 Connecticut Ave., NW
Washington, DC 20009

National School Volunteer Program
601 Wythe Street, Suite 200
Alexandria, VA 22314

Phi Delta Kappa (PDK)
P.O. Box 789
Bloomington, IN 47402-0789

Reading is Fundamental, Inc.
600 Maryland Avenue, SW, Suite 500
Washington, DC 20024

Speech Communication Association
5105 Backlick Road #F
Annandale, VA 22003

Teachers of English to Speakers of Other Languages
1600 Cameron Street, Suite 300
Alexandria, VA 22314-2751

United States Department of Education
400 Maryland Avenue, SW
Washington, DC 20202-7240

Resources and Addresses for Social Studies Teachers

ELECTRONIC BULLETIN BOARD SERVICES:

America Tomorrow Leadership Information
Service (ATLIS)
America Tomorrow, Inc.
P.O. Box 2310
Bethesda, MD 20827-2310
(301) 229-1067
    A condensed source of news and
information on education, community, and
business projects of interest to education leaders;
bulletin-board and mail services; education
database retrieval.

ASCD Access
Association for Supervision & Curriculum
Development (ASCD)
1250 North Pitt Street
Alexandria, VA 22314-1453
(703) 549-9110
    Discussion areas for educators, mail
services, research queries, ASCD product support.

AT&T Learning Network
P.O. Box 4012
Bridgewater, NJ 08807
(800) 367-7225
    Carefully designed curriculum activities
at fixed prices, with strengths in language arts,
social studies, and environmental studies.

CompuServe Inc.
500 Arlington Center Blvd., P.O. Box 20212
Columbus, OH 43220
(800) 848-8199
    The oldest and largest commercial
information utility; online education and
curriculum areas.

FrEdMail (Free Education Mail)
4021 Allen School Road
Bonita, CA 92002
(619) 475-4852
    Over 90 bulletin-board services created by
teachers.

General Electric Information Service
401 N. Washington St.
Rockville, MD 20850
(800) 638-9636
    News retrieval services; same basic
services of CompuServe but with less expensive
on-line rates.

Education Services
8505 Freeport Parkway, Suite 600
Irving, TX 75063
(800) 634-5644
    Umbrella service for a number of
specialized networks including SpecialNet for
special education professionals, Youth News
Service with stories about high school students,
and the ISTEnet online conferencing network
sponsored by the International Society for
Technology in Education.

INTERNET
The Consortium for School Networking
EDUCOM K-12 Networking Project
1112 16th St., NW, Suite 600
Washington, DC 20036
(202) 872-4200
    Platform for Consortium for School
Networking, an ad-hoc group of educators
interested in promoting K-12 networking.

MetaSystems Design Group
P.O. Box 42588
Washington, DC 20015
202) 298-0969
    Highly structured activities for groups,
covering diverse topics, including educational
practice and discussion addressing specific
curriculum topics.

Wayne-Finger Lakes Teacher Resource Center
3501 County Road 20
Stanley, NY 14561
    Grassroots "network" of independent
bulletin board systems operated by schools,
teachers, students, and "friends of education"
sharing information related to K-12 curriculum.

Resources and Addresses for Social Studies Teachers

Learning Link National Consortium
Link Net Inc.
Central Education Network
1400 E. Touhy Ave., Suite 160
Des Plaines, IL 60018
(708) 390-8700
 Lesson plan and classroom activity suggestions keyed to PBS programs, classroom guide to CNN Newsroom.

National Geographic Society Kids Network
Department 90
Washington, DC 20036
(800) 368-2728
 Curriculum activities (for a fee) with an emphasis on the "hard" sciences for elementary school students.

Pals Across the World
4974 S.W. Galen
Lake Oswego, OR 97035
(503) 697-0338
 Electronic "pen pal" service between third-graders and older children, emphasizing writing, poetry, and electronic journalism.

Prodigy Interactive Personal Service
Prodigy Services Co.
445 Hamilton Ave.
White Plains, NY 10615
(800) 776-3449
 Flat monthly fee allowing users to use whatever services they want, any time.

Quantum Computer Services
8619 Westwood Center Drive
Vienna, VA 22182
(800) 227-6364
 Subscription network including teacher forums, an online encyclopedia, tutoring, and a "chat" function in each of its four services.

New York Institute of Technology
Central Islip Campus
Building 66, Room 205
Central Islip, NY 11722
800) 462-9041

Online databases such as ERIC, Facts on File, and a comprehensive medical library; e-mail and electronic bulletin board services.

PERIODICALS FOR CHILDREN:

Calliope
30 Grove Street
Peterborough, NH 03458

Cobblestone
30 Grove Street
Peterborough, NH 03458

Faces
30 Grove Street
Peterborough, NH 03458

Highlights for Children
2300 W. 5th Avenue
Columbus, OH 43272

National Geographic World
National Geographic Society
Washington, DC

Ranger Rick
National Wildlife Foundation
Vienna, VA

FOREIGN EMBASSIES:

Afghanistan
2341 Wyoming Avenue, NW
Washington, DC 20008

Albania
1150 18th Street, NW
Washington, DC 20036

Algeria
2118 Kalorama Road
Washington,DC 20008

Resources and Addresses for Social Studies Teachers

Argentina
1600 New Hampshire Avenue, NW
Washington, DC 20009

Armenia
122 C Street, NW, Suite 360
Washington, DC 20001

Australia
1601 Massachusetts Avenue, NW
Washington, DC 20036

Austria
3524 International Court, NW
Washington, DC 20008

Bahamas
2220 Massachusetts Avenue, NW
Washington, DC 20008

Bahrain
3502 International Drive, NW
Washington, DC 20008

Bangladesh
2201 Wisconsin Avenue, NW, Suite 300
Washington, DC 20007

Barbados
2144 Wyoming Avenue, NW
Washington, DC 20008

Belarus
1511 K Street, NW
Washington, DC 20005

Belgium
3330 Garfield Street, NW
Washington, DC 20008

Belize
2535 Massachusetts Avenue, NW
Washington, DC 20008

Bolivia
3014 Massachusetts Avenue, NW
Washington, DC 20008

Botswana
3400 International Drive, NW
Washington, DC 20008

Brazil
3006 Massachusetts Avenue, NW
Washington, DC 20008

Bulgaria
1621 22nd Street, NW
Washington, DC 20008

Burundi
2233 Wisconsin Avenue, NW
Washington, DC 20007

Cameroon Republic
2349 Massachusetts Avenue, NW
Washington, DC 20008

Canada
501 Pennsylvania Avenue, NW
Washington, DC 20001

Central African Republic
1618 22nd Street, NW
Washington, DC 20008

Chad
2002 R Street, NW
Washington, DC 20008

Chile
1732 Massachusetts Avenue, NW
Washington, DC 20036

China
2300 Connecticut Avenue, NW
Washington, DC 20008

Colombia
2118 Leroy Place, NW
Washington, DC 20008

Costa Rica
1825 Connecticut Avenue, NW
Washington, DC 20009

Resources and Addresses for Social Studies Teachers

Croatia
236 Massachusetts Avenue, NW
Washington, DC 20002

Cuba Mission to the United Nations
315 Lexington Avenue
New York, NY 10016

Cyprus
2211 R Street, NW
Washington, DC 20008

Czech and Slovak Federal Republic
3900 Linnean Avenue, NW
Washington, DC 20008

Denmark
3200 Whitehaven Street, NW
Washington, DC 20008

Djibouti
1156 15th Street, NW
Washington, DC 20005

Dominican Republic
1712 22nd Street, NW
Washington, DC 20008

Ecuador
2535 15th Street, NW
Washington, DC 20009

Egypt
2310 Decatur Place, NW
Washington, DC 20008

El Salvador
2308 California Street, NW
Washington, DC 20008

Equatorial Guinea
57 Magnolia Avenue
Mount Vernon, NY 10553

Ethiopia
2134 Kalorama Road, NW
Washington, DC 20008

Fiji Islands
2233 Wisconsin Avenue, NW
Washington, DC 20007

Finland
3216 New Mexico Avenue, NW
Washington, DC 20016

France
4101 Reservoir Road, NW
Washington, DC 20007

Gabon
2034 20th Street, NW
Washington, DC 20009

Gambia
1155 15th Street, NW
Washington, DC 20005

Germany
4645 Reservoir Road, NW
Washington, DC 20007

Ghana
3512 International Drive, NW
Washington, DC 20008

Greece
2221 Massachusetts Avenue, NW
Washington, DC 20008

Grenada
1701 New Hampshire Avenue, NW
Washington, DC 20009

Guatemala
2220 R Street, NW
Washington, DC 20008

Guinea
2112 Leroy Place, NW
Washington, DC 20008

Guyana
2490 Tracy Place, NW
Washington, DC 20008

Resources and Addresses for Social Studies Teachers

Haiti
2311 Massachusetts Avenue, NW
Washington, DC 20008

Honduras
3007 Tilden Street, NW
Washington, DC 20008

Hungary
3810 Shoemaker Street, NW
Washington, DC 20008

Iceland
2022 Connecticut Avenue, NW
Washington, DC 20008

India
2107 Massachusetts Avenue, NW
Washington, DC 20008

Indonesia
2020 Massachusetts Avenue, NW
Washington, DC 20036

Iran
411 Roosevelt Avenue
Ottawa, ON K2A3X9 Canada

Iraq
215 McLeod Street
Ottawa, ON K2P0Z8 Canada

Ireland
2234 Massachusetts Avenue, NW
Washington, DC 20008

Israel
3514 International Drive, NW
Washington, DC 20008

Italy
1601 Fuller Street, NW
Washington, DC 20009

Ivory Coast
2424 Massachusetts Avenue, NW
Washington, DC 20008

Jamaica
1850 K Street, NW
Washington, DC 20036

Japan
2520 Massachusetts Avenue, NW
Washington, DC 20008

Jordan
3504 International Drive, NW
Washington, DC 20008

Kenya
2249 R Street, NW
Washington, DC 20008

Korea
2450 Massachusetts Avenue, NW
Washington, DC 20008

Kuwait
2940 Tilden Street, NW
Washington, DC 20008

Kyrgyzstan
705 1511 K Street, NW
Washington, DC 20005

Laos
2222 S Street, NW
Washington, DC 20008

Latvia
4325 17th Street, NW
Washington, DC 20011

Lebanon
2560 28th Street, NW
Washington, DC 20008

Lesotho
2511 Massachusetts Avenue, NW
Washington, DC 20008

Liberia
5201 16th Street, NW
Washington, DC 20011

Resources and Addresses for Social Studies Teachers

Lithuania
2622 16th Street, NW
Washington, DC 20009

Luxembourg
2200 Massachusetts Avenue, NW
Washington, DC 20008

Madagascar
2374 Massachusetts Avenue, NW
Washington, DC 20008

Malawi
2408 Massachusetts Avenue, NW
Washington, DC 20008

Malaysia
2401 Massachusetts Avenue, NW
Washington, DC 20008

Maldives Islands Mission to United Nations
820 Second Avenue, Suite 800C
New York, NY 10017

Mali
2130 R Street, NW
Washington, DC 20008

Malta
2017 Connecticut Avenue, NW
Washington, DC 20008

Marshall Islands
2433 Massachusetts Avenue, NW
Washington, DC 20008

Mauritania
2129 Leroy Place, NW
Washington, DC 20008

Mauritius
4301 Connecticut Avenue, NW
Washington, DC 20008

Mexico
1911 Pennsylvania Avenue, NW
Washington, DC 20006

Micronesia
1725 N Street, NW
Washington, DC 20036

Monaco Consulate General
845 Third Avenue
New York, NY 10022

Mongolia
2833 M Street, NW
Washington, DC 20007

Morocco
1601 21st Street, NW
Washington, DC 20009

Namibia
1605 New Hampshire Avenue, NW
Washington, DC 20009

Nepal
2131 Leroy Place, NW
Washington, DC 20008

Netherlands
4200 Linnean Avenue, NW
Washington, DC 20008

New Zealand
37 Observatory Circle, NW
Washington, DC 20008

Nicaragua
1627 New Hampshire Avenue, NW
Washington, DC 20009

Niger
2204 R Street, NW
Washington, DC 20008

Nigeria
2201 M Street, NW
Washington, DC 20037

Norway
2720 34th Street, NW
Washington, DC 20008

Resources and Addresses for Social Studies Teachers

Oman
2342 Massachusetts Avenue, NW
Washington, DC 20008

Pakistan
2315 Massachusetts Avenue, NW
Washington, DC 20008

Panama
2862 McGill Terrace, NW
Washington, DC 20008

Papua New Guinea
1615 New Hampshire Avenue, NW
Washington, DC 20009

Paraguay
2400 Massachusetts Avenue, NW
Washington, DC 20008

Peru
1700 Massachusetts Avenue, NW
Washington, DC 20036

Phillipines
1617 Massachusetts Avenue, NW
Washington, DC 20036

Poland
2640 16th Street, NW
Washington, DC 20009

Portugal
2125 Kalorama Road, NW
Washington, DC 20036

Qatar
600 New Hampshire Avenue, NW
Washington, DC 20037

Romania
1607 23rd Street, NW
Washington, DC 20008

Russia
1125 16th Street, NW
Washington, DC 20036

Rwanda
1714 New Hampshire Avenue, NW
Washington, DC 20009

Saint Lucia
2100 M Street, NW
Washington, DC 20037

Saint Kitts and Nevis
2100 M Street, NW
Washington DC 20037

Saudi Arabia
601 New Hampshire Avenue, NW
Washington, DC 20037

Senegal
2112 Wyoming Avenue, NW
Washington, DC 20008

Seychelles
820 Second Avenue
New York, NY 10017

Sierra Leone
1701 19th Street, NW
Washington, DC 20009

Singapore
1824 R Street, NW
Washington, DC 20009

Slovenia
1300 19th Street, NW
Washington, DC 20036

Somalia
600 New Hampshire Avenue, NW
Washington, DC 20037

South Africa
3051 Massachusetts Avenue, NW
Washington, DC 20008

Spain
2700 15th Street, NW
Washington, DC 20009

Resources and Addresses for Social Studies Teachers

Sri Lanka
2148 Wyoming Avenue, NW
Washington, DC 20008

Sudan
2210 Massachusetts Avenue, NW
Washington, DC 20008

Suriname
4301 Connecticut Avenue, NW
Washington, DC 20008

Swaziland
3400 International Drive, NW
Washington, DC 20008

Sweden
600 New Hampshire Avenue, NW
Washington, DC 20037

Switzerland
2900 Cathedral Avenue, NW
Washington, DC 20008

Syria
2215 Wyoming Avenue, NW
Washington, DC 20008

Taiwan Council for North American Affairs
801 Second Avenue
New York, NY 10017

Tanzania
2139 R Street, NW
Washington, DC 20008

Thailand
2300 Kalorama Road, NW
Washington, DC 20008

Togo
2208 Massachusetts Avenue, NW
Washington, DC 20008

Trinidad & Tobago
1708 Massachusetts Avenue, NW
Washington, DC 20036

Tunisia
1515 Massachusetts Avenue, NW
Washington, DC 20005

Turkey
1714 Massachusetts Avenue, NW
Washington, DC 20036

Uganda
5909 16th Street, NW
Washington, DC 20011

Ukraine
1828 L Street, NW
Washington, DC 20036

United Arab Emirates
600 New Hampshire Avenue, NW
Washington, DC 20037

United Kingdom
3100 Massachusetts Avenue, NW
Washington, DC 20008

Uruguay
1918 F Street, NW
Washington, DC 20006

Vatican City State (Holy See) Nunciature
3339 Massachusetts Avenue, NW
Washington, DC 20008

Venezuela
1099 30th Street, NW
Washington, DC 20007

Yemen
2600 Virginia Avenue, NW
Washington, DC 20037

Yugoslav
2410 California Street, NW
Washington, DC 20008

Zaire
1800 New Hampshire Avenue, NW
Washington, DC 20009

Resources and Addresses for Social Studies Teachers

Zambia
2419 Massachusetts Avenue, NW
Washington, DC 20008

Zimbabwe
1608 New Hampshire Avenue, NW
Washington, DC 20009

PROFESSIONAL ORGANIZATIONS FOR TEACHERS:

American Education Research Association
1230 17th Street, NW
Washington, DC 20036-3078

American Federation of Teachers (AFT)
11 Dupont Circle
Washington, DC 20036

Association for Childhood Education,
International (ACEI)
11141 Georgia Avenue, Suite 200
Wheaton, MD 20902

Association for Supervision and Curriculum
Development (ASCD)
1250 North Pitt Street
Alexandria, VA 22314

Geographic Education National Implementation
Project (GENIP)
1710 16th Street, NW
Washington, DC 20009

International Reading Association (IRA)
800 Barksdale Road
Newark, DE 19711

National Council for Teachers of English (NCTE)
1111 Keyon Road
Urbana, IL 61801

National Council for History Education
26915 Westwood Road, Suite B-2
Westlake, OH 44145-4656

National Council for the Social Studies (NCSS)
3501 Newark Street, NW
Washington, DC 20036

National Council of Mathematics Teachers
1906 Association Drive
Reston, VA 22091

National Education Association (NEA)
1201 16th Street, NW
Washington, DC 20036

National Science Teachers Association
1742 Connecticut Avenue, NW
Washington, DC 20009

Phi Delta Kappa
8th & Union Street
Bloomington, IN 47402

TEN
THEMATIC
STRANDS

Ten Thematic Strands for Teaching Social Studies[1]

The National Council for the Social Studies, founded in 1921, is the nation's largest association devoted exclusively to social studies education. In November 1994, the NCSS released curriculum standards to guide the teaching of social studies from kindergarten through grade twelve. The standards are built around ten thematic strands and were developed after two years of intensive work by the NCSS's National Task Force for Social Studies Standards. The new curriculum standards function as a guide for curriculum development in social studies and are centered around ten thematic strands which incorporate learning experiences from many disciplines.

Strand One: Culture

* *Social studies programs should include experiences that provide for the study of culture and cultural diversity.*

Human beings create, learn, and adapt culture. Culture helps us to understand ourselves as both individuals and members of various groups. Human cultures exhibit both similarities and differences. We all, for example, have systems of beliefs, knowledge, values, and traditions. Each system also is unique. In a democratic and multicultural society, students need to understand multiple perspectives that derive from different cultural vantage points. This understanding will allow them to relate to people in our nation and throughout the world.

Cultures are dynamic and ever changing. The study of culture prepares students to ask and answer questions such as: What are the common characteristics of different cultures? How do belief systems, such as religion or political ideals of the culture, influence the other parts of the culture? How does the culture change to accommodate different ideas and beliefs? What does language tell us about the culture? In schools, this theme typically appears in units and courses dealing with geography, history, and anthropology, as well as multicultural topics across the curriculum.

During the early years of school, the exploration of the concepts of likenesses and differences in school subjects such as language arts, mathematics, science, music, and art makes the study of culture appropriate. Socially, the young learner is beginning to interact with other students, some of whom are like the student and some different; naturally, he or she wants

---

[1] Note: Adapted from *Curriculum Standards for Social Studies: Expectations of Excellence,* 1994, Bulletin 89, National Council for the Social Studies. Used with permission.

to know more about others. In the middle grades, students begin to explore and ask questions about the nature of culture and specific aspects of culture, such as language and beliefs, and the influence of those aspects on human behavior. As students progress through high school, they can understand and use complex cultural concepts such as adaptation, assimilation, acculturation, diffusion, and dissonance drawn from anthropology, sociology, and other disciplines to explain how culture and cultural systems function.

Performance Expectations for Strand One: Culture
- Social studies programs should include experiences that provide for the study of *culture and cultural diversity,* so that the learner can:

Early Grades
a. explore and describe similarities and differences in the ways groups, societies, and cultures address similar human needs and concerns;
b. give examples of ways in which experiences may be interpreted differently by people from diverse cultural perspectives and frames of reference;
c. describe ways in which language, stories, folktales, music, and artistic creations serve as expressions of culture and influence behavior of people living in a particular culture;
d. compare ways in which people from different cultures think about and deal with their physical environment and social conditions;
e. give examples and describe the importance of cultural unity and diversity within and across groups.

Middle Grades
a. compare similarities and differences in the ways groups, societies, and cultures meet human needs and concerns;
b. explain how information and experiences may be interpreted by people from diverse cultural perspectives and frames of reference;
c. explain and give examples of how language, literature, the arts, architecture, other artifacts, traditions, beliefs, values, and behaviors contribute to the development and transmission of culture;
d. explain why individuals and groups respond differently to their physical and social environments and/or changes to these environments on the basis of shared assumptions, values, and beliefs;
e. articulate the implications of cultural diversity, as well as cohesion, within and across groups.

Strand Two: Time, Continuity, & Change

- *Social studies programs should include experiences that provide for the study of the ways human beings view themselves in and over time.*

Human beings seek to understand their historical roots and to locate themselves in time. Such understanding involves knowing what things were like in the past and how things change and develop. Knowing how to read and reconstruct the past allows one to develop a historical perspective and to answer questions such as: Who am I? What happened in the past? How am I connected to those in the past? How has the world changed and how might it change in the future? Why does our personal sense of relatedness to the past change? How can the perspective we have about our own life experiences be viewed as part of the larger human story across time? How do our personal stories reflect varying points of view and inform contemporary ideas and actions?

This theme typically appears in courses that: (1) include perspectives from various aspects of history, (2) draw upon historical knowledge during the examination of social issues, and (3) develop the habits of mind that historians and scholars in the humanities and social sciences employ to study the past and its relationship to the present in the United States and other societies.

Learners in early grades gain experience with sequencing to establish a sense of order and time. They enjoy hearing stories of the recent past as well as of long ago. In addition, they begin to recognize that individuals may hold different views about the past and to understand the linkages between human decisions and consequences. Thus, the foundation is laid for the development of historical knowledge, skills, and values. In the middle grades, students, through a more formal study of history, continue to expand their understanding of the past and of historical concepts and inquiry. They begin to understand and appreciate differences in historical perspectives, recognizing that interpretations are influenced by individual experiences, societal values, and cultural traditions. High school students engage in more sophisticated analysis and reconstruction of the past, examining its relationship to the present and extrapolating into the future. They integrate individual stories about people, events, and situations to form a more holistic conception, in which continuity and change are linked in time and across cultures. Students also learn to draw on their knowledge of history to make informed choices and decisions in the present.

Performance Expectations for Strand Two: Time, Continuity, & Change

- Social studies programs should include experiences that provide for the study of *the ways human beings view themselves in and over time,* so that the learner can:

Early Grades

a. demonstrate an understanding that different people may describe the same event or situation in diverse ways, citing reasons for the differences in views;

b. demonstrate an ability to use correctly vocabulary associated with time, such as past, present, future, and long ago; read and construct simple timelines; identify examples of change; and recognize examples of cause-and-effect relationships;

c. compare and contrast different stories or accounts about past events, people, places, or situations, identifying how they contribute to our understanding of the past;

d. identify and use various sources for reconstructing the past, such as documents, letters, diaries, maps, textbooks, photos, and others;

e. demonstrate and understanding that people in different times and places view the world differently;

f. use knowledge of facts and concepts drawn from history, along with elements of historical inquiry, to inform decision-making about and action taking on public issues.

Middle Grades

a. demonstrate an understanding that different scholars may describe the same event or situation in different ways but must provide reasons or evidence for their views;

b. identify and use key concepts such as chronology, causality, change, conflict, and complexity to explain, analyze, and show connections among patterns of historical change and continuity;

c. identify and describe selected historical periods and patterns of change within and across cultures, such as the rise of civilizations, the development of transportation systems, the growth and breakdown of colonial systems, and others;

d. identify and use processes important to reconstructing and reinterpreting the past, such as using a variety of sources; providing, validating, and weighing evidence for claims; checking credibility of sources; and searching for causality;

e. develop critical sensitivities such as empathy and skepticism regarding attitudes, values, and behaviors of people in different historical contexts;

f. use knowledge of facts and concepts drawn from history, along with methods of historical inquiry, to inform decision making about and action taking on public issues.

Strand Three: People, Places, & Environments
- *Social studies programs should include experiences that provide for the study of people, places, and environments.*

Technological advances connect students at all levels to the world beyond their personal locations. The study of people, places, and human-environment interactions assists learners as they create their spatial views and geographic perspectives of the world. Today's social, cultural, economic, and civic demands on individuals mean that students will need the knowledge, skills, and understanding to ask and answer questions such as: Where are things located? Why are they located where they are? What patterns are reflected in the groupings of things? What do we mean by region? How do landforms change? What implications do these changes have for people? This area of study helps learners make informed and critical decisions about the relationship between human beings and their environment. In schools, this theme typically appears in units and courses dealing with area studies and geography.

In the early grades, young learners draw upon immediate personal experiences as a basis for exploring geographic concepts and skills. They also express interest in things distant and unfamiliar and have concern for the use and abuse of the physical environment. During the middle school years, students relate their personal experiences to happenings in other environmental contexts. Appropriate experiences will encourage increasingly abstract thought as students use data and apply skills in analyzing human behavior in relation to its physical and cultural environment. Students in high school are able to apply geographic understanding across a broad range of fields, inducing the fine arts, sciences, and humanities. Geographic concepts become central to learners' comprehension of global connections as they expand their knowledge of diverse cultures, both historical and contemporary. The importance of core geographic themes to public policy is recognized and should be explored as students address issues of domestic and international significance.

Performance Expectations for Strand Three: Peoples, Places, & Environments
- Social studies programs should include experiences that provide for the study of *people, places, and environments,* so that the learner can:

Early Grades

a. construct and use mental maps of locales, regions, and the world that demonstrate understanding of relative location, direction, size, and shape;

b. interpret, use, and distinguish various representations of the Earth, such as maps, globes, and photographs;

c. use appropriate resources, data sources, and geographic tools such as atlases, data bases, grid systems, charts, graphs, and maps to generate, manipulate, and interpret information;

d. estimate distance and calculate scale;

e. locate and distinguish among varying landforms and geographic features, such as mountains, plateaus, islands, and oceans;

f. describe and speculate about physical system changes, such as seasons, climate and weather, and the water cycle;

g. describe how people create places that reflect ideas, personality, culture, and wants and needs as they design homes, playgrounds, classrooms, and the like;

h. examine the interaction of human beings and their physical environment, the use of land, building of cities, and ecosystem changes in selected locales and regions;

i. explore ways that the Earth's physical features have changed over time in the local region and beyond and how these changes may be connected to one another;

j. observe and speculate about social and economic effects of environmental changes and crises resulting from phenomena such as floods, storms, and drought;

k. consider existing uses and propose and evaluate alternative uses of resources and land in home, school, community, the region, and beyond.

Middle Grades

a. elaborate mental maps of locales, regions, and the world that demonstrate understanding of relative location, direction, size, and shape;

b. create, interpret, use, and distinguish various representations of the Earth, such as maps, globes, and photographs;

c. use appropriate resources, data sources, and geographic tools such as aerial photographs, satellite images, geographic information systems (GIS), map projections, and cartography to generate, manipulate, and interpret information such as atlases, data bases, grid systems, charts, graphs, and maps;

d. estimate distance, calculate scale, and distinguish other geographic relationships such as population density and spatial distribution patterns;

e. locate and describe varying landforms and geographic features, such as mountains, plateaus, islands, rain forests, deserts, and oceans, and explain their relationships within the ecosystem;

f. describe physical system changes such as seasons, climate and weather, and the water cycle and identify geographic patterns associated with them;

g. describe how people create places that reflect cultural values and ideals as they build neighborhoods, parks, shopping centers, and the like;

h. examine, interpret, and analyze physical and cultural patterns and their interactions, such as land use, settlement patterns, cultural transmission of customs and ideas, and ecosystem changes;

i. describe ways that historical events have been influenced by, and have influenced, physical and human geographic factors in local, regional, national, and global settings;

j. observe and speculate about social and economic effects of environmental changes and crises resulting from phenomena such as floods, storms, and drought;

k. propose, compare, and evaluate alternative uses of land and resources in communities, regions, nations, and the world.

Strand Four: Individual Development & Identity

- *Social studies programs should include experiences that provide for the study of individual development and identity.*

Personal identity is shaped by one's culture, by groups, and by institutional influences. How do people learn? Why do people behave as they do? What influences how people learn, perceive, and grow? How do people meet their basic needs in a variety of contexts? Questions such as these are central to the study of how individuals develop from youth to adulthood. Examination of various forms of human behavior enhances understanding of the relationships among social norms and emerging personal identities, the social processes that influence identity formation, and the ethical principles underlying individual action. In schools, this theme typically appears in units and courses dealing with psychology and anthropology.

Given the nature of individual development and our own cultural context, students need to be aware of the processes of learning, growth, and development at every level of their school experience. In the early grades, for example, observing brothers, sisters, and older adults; looking at family photo albums; remembering past achievements and projecting oneself into the future; and comparing the patterns of behavior evident in people of different age groups are appropriate activities because young learners develop their personal identities in the context of families, peers, schools, and communities. Central to this development are the exploration, identification, and analysis of how individuals relate to others. In the middle grades, issues of personal identity are refocused as the individual begins to explain self in relation to others in the society and culture. At the high school level, students need to encounter multiple opportunities to examine contemporary patterns of human behavior, using methods from the behavioral sciences to apply core concepts drawn from psychology, social psychology, sociology, and anthropology as the apply to individuals, societies, and cultures.

Performance Expectations for Strand Four: Individual Development & Identity

- Social studies programs should include experiences that provide for the study of *individual development and identity,* so that the learner can:

Early Grades
a. describe personal changes over time, such as those related to physical development and personal interests;
b. describe personal connections to place—especially place as associated with immediate surroundings;
c. describe the unique features of one's nuclear and extended families;
d. show how learning and physical development affect behavior;
e. identify and describe ways family, groups, and community influence the individual's daily life and personal choices;
f. explore factors that contribute to one's personal identity, such as interests, capabilities, and perceptions;
g. analyze a particular event to identify reasons individuals might respond to it in different ways;
h. work independently and cooperatively to accomplish goals.

Middle Grades
a. relate personal changes to social, cultural, and historical contexts;
b. describe personal connections to place—as associated with community, nation, and world;
c. describe the ways family, gender, ethnicity, nationality, and institutional affiliations contribute to personal identity;
d. relate such factors as physical endowment and capabilities, learning, motivation, personality, perception, and behavior to individual development;
e. identify and describe ways regional, ethnic, and national cultures

influence individuals' daily lives;
f. identify and describe the influence of perception, attitudes, values, and beliefs on personal identity;
g. identify and interpret examples of stereotyping, conformity, and altruism;
h. work independently and cooperatively to accomplish goals.

Strand Five: Individuals, Groups, & Institutions
* *Social studies programs should include experiences that provide for the study of interactions among individuals, groups, and institutions.*

Institutions such as schools, churches, families, government agencies, and the courts all play an integral role in our lives. These and other institutions exert enormous influence over us, yet institutions are no more than organizational embodiments to further the core social values of those who comprise them. Thus, it is important that students know how institutions are formed, what controls and influences them, how they control and influence individuals and culture, and how institutions can be maintained or changed. The study of individuals, groups, and institutions, drawing upon sociology, anthropology, and other disciplines, prepares students to ask and answer questions such as: What is the role of institutions in this and other societies? How am I influenced by institutions? How do institutions change? What is my role in institutional change? In schools, this theme typically appears in units and courses dealing with sociology, anthropology, psychology, political science, and history.

Young children should be given opportunities to examine various institutions that affect their lives and influence their thinking. They should be assisted in recognizing the tensions that occur when the goals, values, and principles of two or more institutions or groups conflict—for example, when the school board prohibits candy machines in schools versus a class project to install a candy machine to help raise money for the local hospital. They should also have opportunities to explore ways in which institutions such as churches or health care networks are created to respond to changing individual and group needs. Middle school learners will benefit from varied experiences through which they examine the ways in which institutions change over time, promote social conformity, and influence culture. They should be encouraged to use this understanding to suggest ways to work through institutional change for the common good. high school students must understand the paradigms and traditions that undergird social and political institutions. They should be provided opportunities to examine, use, and add to the body of knowledge related to the behavioral sciences and social theory as it relates to the ways people and groups organize themselves around common needs, beliefs, and interests.

Performance Expectations for Strand Five: Individuals, Groups, & Institutions
• Social studies programs should include experiences that provide for the study of *interactions among individuals, groups, and institutions,* so that the learner can:

Early Grades
a. identify roles as learned behavior patterns in group situations, such as student, family member, peer play group member, or club member;
b. give examples of and explain group and institutional influences such as religious beliefs; laws; and peer pressure on people, events, and elements of culture;
c. identify examples of institutions and describe the interactions of people with institutions;
d. identify and describe examples of tensions between and among individuals, groups, or institutions, and the ways in which belonging to more than one group can cause internal conflicts;
e. identify and describe examples of tension between an individual's beliefs and government policies and laws;
f. give examples of the role of institutions in furthering both continuity and change;
g. show how groups and institutions work to meet individual needs and promote the common good, and identify examples of where they fail to do so.

Middle Grades
a. demonstrate an understanding of concepts such as role, status, and social class in describing the interactions of individuals and social groups;
b. analyze group and institutional influences on people, events, and elements of culture;
c. describe the various forms institutions take and the interactions of people with institutions;
d. identify and analyze examples of tensions between expressions of individuality and group or institutional efforts to promote social conformity;
e. identify and describe examples of tensions between belief systems and government policies and laws;
f. describe the role of institutions in furthering both continuity and change;
g. apply knowledge of how groups and institutions work to meet individual

needs and promote the common good.

Strand Six: Power, Authority, & Governance
- *Social studies programs should include experiences that provide for the study of the ways in which people create and change structures of power, authority, and governance.*

Understanding the historical development of structures of power, authority, and governance and their evolving functions in contemporary U. S. society, as well as in other parts of the world, is essential for developing civic competence. In exploring this theme, students confront questions such as: What is power? What forms does it take? Who holds it? How is it gained, used, and justified? What is legitimate authority? How are governments created, structured, maintained, and changed? How can we keep government responsive to its citizens' needs and interests? How can individual rights be protected within the context of majority rule? by examining the purposes and characteristics of various governance systems, learners develop an understanding of the ways in which groups and nations attempt to resolve conflicts and seek to establish order and security. Through study of the dynamic relationships among individual rights and responsibilities, the needs of social groups, and concepts of a just society, learners become more effective problem solvers and decision makers when addressing the persistent issues and social problems encountered in public life. They do so by applying concepts and methods of political science and law. In schools, this theme typically appears in units and courses dealing with government, politics, political science, history, law, and other social sciences.

Learners in the early grades explore their natural and developing sense of fairness and order as they experience relationships with others. They develop an increasingly comprehensive awareness of rights and responsibilities in specific contexts. During the middle school years, these rights and responsibilities are reapplied in more complex contexts with emphasis on new applications. High school students develop their abilities in the use of abstract principles. They study the various systems that have been developed over the centuries to allocate and employ power and authority in the governing process. At every level, learners should have opportunities to apply their knowledge and skills to and participate in the workings of the various levels of power, authority, and governance.

Performance Expectations for Strand Six: Power, Authority, & Governance
• Social studies programs should include experiences that provide for the study of *the ways in which people create and change structures of power, authority, and governance,* so that the learner can:

Early Grades
a. examine the rights and responsibilities of the individual in relation to his or her social group, such as family, peer group, and school class;
b. explain the purpose of government;
c. give examples of the ways in which government does or does not provide for needs and wants of people, establish order and security, and manage conflict;
d. recognize the ways in which groups and organizations encourage unity and deal with diversity to maintain order and security;
e. distinguish among local, state, and national government and identify representative leaders at these levels, such as mayor, governor, and president;
f. identify and describe factors that contribute to cooperation and cause disputes within and among groups and nations;
g. explore the role of technology in communications, transportation, information processing, weapons development, or other areas as it contributes to or helps resolve conflicts;
h. recognize and give examples of the tensions between the wants and needs of individuals and groups, and concepts such as fairness, equity, and justice.

Middle Grades
a. examine persistent issues involving the rights, roles, and status of the individual in relation to the general welfare;
b. describe the purpose of government and how its powers are acquired, used, and justified;
c. analyze and explain ideas and governmental mechanisms to meet needs and wants of citizens, regulate territory, manage conflict, and establish order and security;
d. describe the ways nations and organizations respond to forces of unity and diversity affecting order and security;
e. identify and describe the basic features of the political system in the United States, and identify representative leaders from various levels and branches of government;
f. explain conditions, actions, and motivations that contribute to conflict and cooperation within and among nations;
g. describe and analyze the role of technology in communications, transportation, information processing, weapons development, or other

areas as it contributes to or helps resolve conflicts;
h. explain and apply concepts such as power, role, status, justice, and
influence to the examination of persistent issues and social problems;
i. give examples and explain the ways in which governments attempt to
achieve their stated ideals at home and abroad.

Strand Seven: Production, Distribution, & Consumption

- *Social studies programs should include experiences that provide for
  the study of the ways in which people organize for the production,
  distribution, and consumption of goods and services.*

People have wants that often exceed the limited resources available to
them. As a result, a variety of ways have been invented to decide upon
answers to four fundamental questions: What is to be produced? How is
production to be organized? How are goods and services to be distributed?
What is the most effective allocation of the factors of production (land, labor,
capital, and management)? Unequal distribution of resources necessitates
systems of exchange, including trade, to improve the well-being of the
economy, while the role of government in economic policymaking varies
over time and from place to place. Increasingly, these decisions are global in
scope and require systematic study of an interdependent world economy and
the role of technology in economic decision making. In schools, this theme
typically appears in units and courses dealing with concepts, principles, and
issues drawn from the discipline of economics.

Young learners begin by differentiating between wants and needs.
They explore economic decisions as they compare their own economic
experiences with those of others and consider the wider consequences of
those decisions on groups, communities, the nation, and beyond. In the
middle grades, learners expand their knowledge of economic concepts and
principles, and use economic reasoning processes in addressing issues related
to the four fundamental economic questions. High school students develop
economic perspectives and deeper understanding of key economic concepts
and processes through systematic study of a range of economic and
sociopolitical systems, with particular emphasis on the examination of
domestic and global economic policy options related to matters such as health
care, resource use, unemployment, and trade.

Performance Expectations for Strand Seven: Production, Distribution, & Consumption
- Social studies programs should include experiences that provide for the study of *the ways in which people organize for the production, distribution, and consumption of goods and services,* so that the learner can:

Early Grades
a. give examples that show how scarcity and choice govern our economic decisions;
b. distinguish between needs and wants;
c. identify examples of private and public goods and services;
d. give examples of the various institutions that make up economic systems such as families, workers, banks, labor unions, government agencies, small businesses, and large corporations;
e. describe how we depend upon workers with specialized jobs and the ways in which they contribute to the production and exchange of goods and services;
f. describe the influence of incentives, values, traditions, and habits on economic decisions;
g. explain and demonstrate the role of money in everyday life;
h. describe the relationship of price to supply and demand;
i. use economic concepts such as supply, demand, and price to help explain events in the community and nation;
j. apply knowledge of economic concepts in developing a response to a current local economic issue, such as how to reduce the flow of trash into a rapidly filling landfill.

Middle Grades
a. give and explain examples of ways that economic systems structure choices about how goods and services are to be produced and distributed;
b. describe the role that supply and demand, prices, incentives, and profits play in determining what is produced and distributed in a competitive market system;
c. explain the difference between private and public goods and services;
d. describe a range of examples of the various institutions that make up economic systems, such as households, business firms, banks, government agencies, labor unions, and corporations;
e. describe the role of specialization and exchange in the economic process;
f. explain and illustrate how values and beliefs influence different economic decisions;

__g.__ differentiate among various forms of exchange and money;
__h.__ compare basic economic systems according to who determines what is
produced, distributed, and consumed;
__i.__ use economic concepts to help explain historical and current
developments and issues in local, national, or global contexts;
__j.__ use economic reasoning to compare different proposals for dealing with a
contemporary social issue such as unemployment, acid rain, or high quality
education.

Strand Eight: Science, Technology, & Society

- *Social studies programs should include experiences that provide for the study of relationships among science, technology, and society.*

Technology is as old as the first crude tool invented by prehistoric
humans, but today's technology forms the basis for some of our most difficult
social choices. Modern life as we know it would be impossible without
technology and the science that supports it. However, technology brings with
it many questions: Is new technology always better than that which it will
replace? What can we learn from the past about how new technologies result
in broader social change, some of which is unanticipated? How can we cope
with the ever-increasing pace of change, perhaps even with the feeling that
technology has gotten out of control? How can we manage technology so
that the greatest number of people benefit from it? How can we preserve our
fundamental values and beliefs in a world that is rapidly becoming one
technology-linked village? This theme appears in units or courses dealing
with history, geography, economics, and civics and government. It draws
upon several scholarly fields from the natural and physical sciences, social
sciences, and the humanities for specific examples of issues and the
knowledge base for considering responses to the societal issues related to
science and technology.

Young children can learn how technologies form systems and how
their daily lives are intertwined with a host of technologies. They can study
how basic technologies such as ships, automobiles, and airplanes have
evolved and how we have employed technology such as air conditioning,
dams, and irrigation to modify our physical environment. From history
(their own and others'), they can construct examples of how technologies
such as the wheel, the stirrup, and the transistor radio altered the course of
history. By the middle grades, students can begin to explore the complex
relationships among technology, human values, and behavior. They will

find that science and technology bring changes that surprise us and even challenge our beliefs, as in the case of discoveries and their applications related to our universe, the genetic basis of life, atomic physics, and others. As they move from middle grades to high school, students will need to think more deeply about how we can manage technology so that we control it rather than the other way around. There should be opportunities to confront such issues as the consequences of using robots to produce goods, the protection of privacy in the age of computers and electronic surveillance, and the opportunities and challenges of genetic engineering, test-tube life, and medical technology, with all their implications for longevity, quality of life, and religious beliefs.

Performance Expectations for Strand Eight: Science, Technology, & Society

- Social studies programs should include experiences that provide for the study of *relationships among science, technology, and society*, so that the learner can:

Early Grades
a. identify and describe examples in which science and technology have changed the lives of people, such as in homemaking, childcare, work, transportation, and communication;

b. identify and describe examples in which science and technology have led to changes in the physical environment, such as the building of dams and levees, offshore oil drilling, medicine from rain forests, and loss of rain forests due to extraction of resources or alternative uses;

c. describe instances in which changes in values, beliefs, and attitudes have resulted from new scientific and technological knowledge, such as conservation of resources and awareness of chemicals harmful to life and the environment;

d. identify examples of laws and policies that govern scientific and technological applications, such as the Endangered Species Act and environmental protection policies;

e. suggest ways to monitor science and technology in order to protect the physical environment, individual rights, and the common good.

Middle Grades
a. examine and describe the influence of culture on scientific and technological choices and advancement, such as transportation, medicine, and warfare;

b. show through specific examples how science and technology have changed people's perceptions of the social and natural world, such as in their relationship to the land, animal life, family life, and economic needs, wants, and security.

c. describe examples in which values, beliefs, and attitudes have been influenced by new scientific and technological knowledge, such as the invention of the printing press, conceptions of the universe, applications of atomic energy, and genetic discoveries;

d. explain the need for laws and policies to govern scientific and technological applications, such as in the safety and well-being of workers and consumers and the regulation of utilities, radio, and television;

e. seek reasonable and ethical solutions to problems that arise when scientific advancements and social norms or values come into conflict.

Strand Nine: Global Connections

- *Social studies programs should include experiences that provide for the study of global connections and interdependence.*

The realities of global interdependence require an understanding of the increasingly important and diverse global connections among world societies. Analysis of tensions between national interests and global priorities contributes to the development of possible solutions to persistent and emerging global issues in many fields: health care, economic development, environmental quality, universal human rights, and others. Analyzing patterns and relationships within and among world cultures, such as economic competition and interdependence, age-old ethnic enmities, political and military alliances, and others, helps learners carefully examine policy alternatives that have both national and global implications. This theme typically appears in units or courses dealing with geography, culture, and economics, but again can draw upon the natural and physical sciences and the humanities, including literature, the arts, and language.

Through exposure to various media and firsthand experiences, young learners become aware of and are affected by events on a global scale. Within this context, students in early grades examine and explore global connections and basic issues and concerns, suggesting and initiating responsive action plans. In the middle years, learners can initiate analysis of the interactions among states and nations and their cultural complexities as they respond to global events and changes. At the high school level, students are able to think systematically about personal, national, and global decisions, interactions, and consequences, including addressing critical issues such as peace, human rights, trade, and global ecology.

Performance Expectations for Strand Nine: Global Connections
- Social studies programs should include experiences that provide for the study of *global connections and interdependence,* so that the learner can:

Early Grades
a. explore ways that language, art, music, belief systems, and other cultural elements may facilitate global understanding or lead to misunderstanding;
b. give examples of conflict, cooperation, and interdependence among individuals, groups, and nations;
c. examine the effects of changing technologies on the global community;
d. explore causes, consequences, and possible solutions to persistent, contemporary, and emerging global issues, such as pollution and endangered species;
e. examine the relationships and tensions between personal wants and needs and various global concerns, such as use of imported oil, land use, and environmental protection;
f. investigate concerns, issues, standards, and conflicts related to universal human rights, such as the treatment of children, religious groups, and effects of war.

Middle Grades
a. describe instances in which language, art, music, belief systems, and other cultural elements can facilitate global understanding or cause misunderstanding;
b. analyze examples of conflict, cooperation, and interdependence among groups, societies, and nations;
c. describe and analyze the effects of changing technologies on the global community;
d. explore the causes, consequences, and possible solutions to persistent, contemporary, and emerging global issues, such as health, security, resource allocation, economic development, and environmental quality;
e. describe and explain the relationships and tensions between national sovereignty and global interests in such matters as territory, natural resources, trade, use of technology, and welfare of people;
f. demonstrate understanding of concerns, standards, issues, and conflicts related to universal human rights;
g. identify and describe the roles of international and multinational organizations.

Strand Ten: Civic Ideals & Practices
- *Social studies programs should include experiences that provide for the study of the ideals, principles, and practices of citizenship in a democratic republic.*

An understanding of civic ideals and practices of citizenship is critical to full participation in society and is a central purpose of the social studies. All people have a stake in examining civic ideals and practices across time and in diverse societies as well as at home, and in determining how to close the gap between present practices and the ideals upon which our democratic republic is based. Learners confront such questions as: What is civic participation and how can I be involved? How has the meaning of citizenship evolved? What is the balance between rights and responsibilities? What is the role of the citizen in the community and the nation, and as a member of the world community? How can I make a positive difference? In schools, this theme typically appears in units or courses dealing with history, political science, cultural anthropology, and fields such as global studies and law-related education, while also drawing upon content from the humanities.

In the early grades, students are introduced to civic ideals and practices through activities such as helping to set classroom expectations, examining experiences in relation to ideals, and determining how to balance the needs of individuals and the group. During these years, children also experience views of citizenship in other times and places through stories and drama. By the middle grades, students expand their ability to analyze and evaluate the relationships between ideals and practice. They are able to see themselves taking civic roles in their communities. High school students increasingly recognize the rights and responsibilities of citizens in identifying societal needs, setting directions for public policies, and working to support both individual dignity and the common good. They learn by experience how to participate in community service and political activities and how to use democratic process to influence public policy.

Performance Expectations for Strand Ten: Civic Ideals & Practices
- Social studies programs should include experiences that provide for the study of *the ideals, principles, and practices of citizenship in a democratic republic,* so that the learner can:

Early Grades
a. identify key ideals of the United States' democratic-republican form of

government, such as individual human dignity, liberty, justice, equality, and the rule of law, and discuss their application in specific situations;
b. identify examples of rights and responsibilities of citizens;
c. locate, access, organize, and apply information about an issue of public concern from multiple points of view;
d. identify and practice selected forms of civic discussion and participation consistent with the ideals of citizens in a democratic republic;
e. explain actions citizens can take to influence public policy decisions;
f. recognize that a variety of formal and informal actors influence and shape public policy;
g. examine the influence of public opinion on personal decision making and government policy on public issues;
h. explain how public policies and citizen behaviors may or may not reflect the stated ideals of a democratic-republican form of government;
i. describe how public policies are used to address issues of public concern;
j. recognize and interpret how the "common good" can be strengthened through various forms of citizen action.

Middle Grades
a. examine the origins and continuing influence of key ideals of the democratic-republican form of government, such as individual human dignity, liberty, justice, equality, and the rule of law;
b. identify and interpret sources and examples of the rights and responsibilities of citizens;
c. locate, access, analyze, organize, and apply information about selected public issues—recognizing and explaining multiple points of view;
d. practice forms of civic discussion and participation consistent with the ideals of citizens in a democratic republic;
e. explain and analyze various forms of citizen action that influence public policy decisions;
f. identify and explain the roles of formal and informal political actors in influencing and shaping public policy and decision making;
g. analyze the influence of diverse forms of public opinion on the development of public policy and decision making;
h. analyze the effectiveness of selected public policies and citizen behaviors in realizing the stated ideals of a democratic-republican form of government;
i. explain the relationship between policy statements and action plans used to address issues of public concern;
j. examine strategies designed to strengthen the "common good," which consider a range of options for citizen action.

Creating
Lesson Plans
and
Unit Plans

Lesson Plans

Almost all teachers make plans for teaching. Sometimes the plans exist only in the teacher's mind and sometimes the plans are carefully written, but in any case, they provide an arrangement of events for instructional delivery.

A lesson plan is the teacher's trip map through the lesson. It is a guide to remind the teacher of the sequence of events planned for a lesson. Many designs for lesson plans exist, but it is the work of the late Madeline Hunter that appears most often in lesson-plan design. Hunter said that a lesson plan, to be effective, should:

- establish an anticipatory set,
- communicate the lesson's objectives,
- provide direct instruction,
- model the processes to be learned,
- check for understanding,
- provide meaningful guided practice, and
- provide independent activity or practice.

Hunter recognized that all steps do not necessarily appear in all lessons. The sequence, for example, may extend over several lessons, and Hunter pointed out that the order of the steps should be varied to fit the needs of the pupils and the subject matter at hand. In planning lessons, however, Hunter suggested that teachers consider each of the seven elements and think in terms of an anticipatory set (the beginning of the lesson), an instructional/modeling sequence (the middle of the lesson), and a concluding set (the ending of the lesson).

In the following two examples of lesson plan formats, Lesson Plan One represents the Hunter model rather closely. It is fairly detailed and breaks down the elements of the lesson more exactly. Lesson Plan Two is a modification that is shorter and briefer. It is less detailed and easier to follow. The plans for the activities in this book follow the model depicted in Lesson Plan Two.

Lesson Plan One

Date: (date of lesson)   **Grade:** (usually a span of suggested grade levels)

Topic: (a descriptive title)   **Major Concepts:** (big ideas to be presented)

Materials Needed:
(enumerated listing of the materials needed to teach the lesson)

Objectives: **Time:**
(some behavioral, some general)   (approximate lesson length)

Introduction to Lesson

1.   **Anticipatory Set:**
     (focus pupils, establish transfer)
2.   **Purpose:**
     (state purpose and objectives)

Major Instructional Sequence

3.   **Instruction:**
     (provide information, explain concepts, state definitions, etc.)
4.   **Modeling:**
     (provide examples)
5.   **Checking for Understanding:**
     (pose key questions; ask pupils to generate examples and explain concepts, definitions, and attributes in own words)

Concluding Sequence

6.   **Guided Practice:**
     (initiate practice activities which are under direct teacher supervision, elicit overt responses that demonstrate behavior, circulate and provide close monitoring, provide feedback of results)
7.   **Independent Practice:**
     (have pupils continue to practice on their own and provide them with knowledge of results)

Evaluation/Closure

(final assessment to determine if pupils have met objectives)

Lesson Plan Two

Topic:
(a descriptive title)

Grade Level: **Time:**
(usually a span of suggested grade levels)   (approximate length of lesson)

Materials Needed:
(enumerated listing of the materials needed to teach the lesson)
1.
2.
etc.

Objectives:
(some behavioral; some general)
1.
2.
etc.

Introduction:
(getting attention)
1.
2.
etc.

Major Instructional Sequence:
(modeling; giving instruction; discussion; checking for understanding; guided practice)
1.
2.
etc.

Closure or Evaluation:
(final assessment to determine if pupils have met objectives)

Unit Plans

It is often very worthwhile to plan a series of lessons around a central idea, or theme, creating a thematic unit. Units can be of short duration, lasting only two or three days, or they can be much longer, lasting as long as three or more weeks. Very often, units are integrational in that they incorporate skills and content from different subject areas.

Teachers with several years of experience will recognize that the thematic unit approach to teaching is not new. They perhaps remember when it was called the unit method and was first introduced to them during their teacher preparation days in college during the late 1950s, the 1960s, and the 1970s. In the 1980s, however, a fragmented curriculum became the vogue, and the unit approach became frowned upon and fell into disfavor. But in the 1990s, thematic units began resurging. Today, thematic units are becoming the heart of social studies programs in the elementary school.

While daily lesson plans form the major part of a unit, unit plans are more than just a collection of daily lesson plans. Unit plans contain components which make the lessons coalesce and meld around the central theme and add functionality to the unit. A good unit should contain a descriptive title, the intended grade level, a table of contents, some background information for the teacher, unit objectives, suggestions for initiating the unit, a list of learning activities, a list of materials needed for the unit, lesson plans for each day of the unit, sketches of bulletin-board ideas, the way the unit is to be evaluated, and a bibliography of both books for pupils and references for teachers.

The following section presents a description of the components for a unit plan (page 11.5), ideas for selecting topics for themes in primary and intermediate grades (page 11.6), a themeweb showing the curriculum integration occurring in a unit on the environment (page 11.7), a description of goals and objectives (page 11.8), an evaluation form for use with students making lesson presentations in method's classes (page 11.9), eight vital topics in social studies today (page 11.10), grouping strategies in social studies (page 11.11), the importance of using all modalities of learning when planning lessons and units (page 11.12), strategies for using questioning (page 11.13), a descriptive outline of Benjamin Bloom's educational objectives (page 11.14), and a chart of key words in questioning which correlate with Bloom's cognitive levels (page 11.15).

COMPONENTS OF A UNIT PLAN

TITLE
   A topic or problem such as The Middle East, Festivals of Mexico, The Cajuns of Louisiana, Rivers of North America, Environmental Protection, and the like.

GRADE LEVEL
   Usually a range of appropriate grade levels.

TABLE OF CONTENTS
   A listing of the unit's contents with numbered pages.

BACKGROUND INFORMATION
   The rationale for the unit. An overview of content, main ideas, and concepts.

OBJECTIVES
   Expected knowledge and skill outcomes, both general and behavioral.

INITIATION
   Suggestions for beginning the unit in an interesting, distinctive way.

LIST OF LEARNING ACTIVITIES
   Introductory activities to focus attention, developmental activities to provide for intake and application of content, and concluding activities to reiterate main ideas and culminate the unit.

LIST OF MATERIALS NEEDED FOR UNIT
   An enumerated list of the materials needed in the lessons of the unit.

DAILY LESSON PLANS
   Plans for each day in the unit (see pages 11.2 and 11.3).

BULLETIN-BOARD SKETCHES
   Small sketches of ideas for appropriate bulletin boards.

EVALUATION
   Suggestions, tests, and the like for assessing learning in the unit.

BIBLIOGRAPHY
   Books for pupils and references for the teacher are included.

Ideas for Selecting Thematic Topics

Adapted from Meinbach, A., Rothlein, L., & Fredericks, A. (1995). *The Complete Guide to Thematic Units: Creating the Integrated Curriculum.* (Pages 9-10). Norwood, MA: Christopher-Gordon Publishers, Inc. Used with permission.

Theme Topics	Primary (Grades 1-3)	Intermediate (Grades 3-6)
Curricular Areas	Animals The seasons Dinosaurs Weather Plants Staying healthy The changing Earth Sun and moon Magnetism Simple machines Light and heat Neighborhoods Communities Transportation Growing up Family life Holidays Celebrations Sports Native Americans	Body system Inventors The environment Oceanography Life cycles Work and energy Electricity Sound and light Solar system The changing Earth Space Mythology Geography Discovery Becoming a nation Pioneer life War and peace Multiculturalism Careers Ancient cultures
Issues	Homework Family matters Siblings Trash disposal Rules	Pollution Water quality Toxic wastes Air quality Nuclear power
Problems	Energy use Crime Natural resources The environment Food	Ozone layer Starvation Population Oil spills Wildlife Solar power
Special Events	Birthdays Winter holidays Circus Field trip Olympics Summer vacation	Shuttle launch Elections World Series Super Bowl Unusual weather Legislation
Pupil Interests	Dinosaurs Monsters Sharks Airplanes Friends and neighbors Vacations Space exploration Ocean creatures Scary things	Computers Famous people Ecology Environment Sports heroes/heroines Sports Relationships Clothes Vacations

Sample Themeweb Planning Form

Adapted from Meinbach, A., Rothlein, L., & Fredericks, A. (1995). *The Complete Guide to Thematic Units: Creating the Integrated Curriculum.* (Page 12). Norwood, MA: Christopher-Gordon Publishers, Inc. Used with permission.

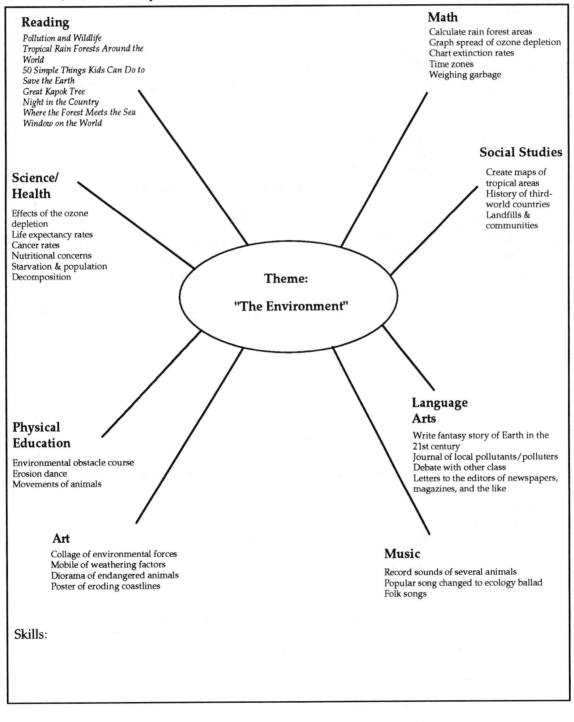

Reading

Pollution and Wildlife
Tropical Rain Forests Around the World
50 Simple Things Kids Can Do to Save the Earth
Great Kapok Tree
Night in the Country
Where the Forest Meets the Sea
Window on the World

Math

Calculate rain forest areas
Graph spread of ozone depletion
Chart extinction rates
Time zones
Weighing garbage

Science/ Health

Effects of the ozone depletion
Life expectancy rates
Cancer rates
Nutritional concerns
Starvation & population
Decomposition

Social Studies

Create maps of tropical areas
History of third-world countries
Landfills & communities

Theme:

"The Environment"

Physical Education

Environmental obstacle course
Erosion dance
Movements of animals

Language Arts

Write fantasy story of Earth in the 21st century
Journal of local pollutants/polluters
Debate with other class
Letters to the editors of newspapers, magazines, and the like

Art

Collage of environmental forces
Mobile of weathering factors
Diorama of endangered animals
Poster of eroding coastlines

Music

Record sounds of several animals
Popular song changed to ecology ballad
Folk songs

Skills:

DIFFERENTIATING BETWEEN GOALS AND OBJECTIVES

Goals are the broad purposes of social studies. They are pervasive and transcend the aims of daily lesson plans. Goals provide the basic rationale and main charge of social studies in the school curriculum.

Objectives, on the other hand, represent changes that are expected to take place in pupils on a daily basis as a result of lessons.

Examples of traditional goals of social studies programs in American education include:

- **Active, informed citizenship.**
- **Enlightened patriotism.**
- **Development of critical thought.**
- **Tolerance in accepting and respecting other peoples' cultures.**

Behavioral objectives are used to define the specific terminal traits expected after a teaching episode. The use of behavioral objectives in lesson plans was given impetus by the clamor for accountability and the requirements for governmental grants. (Note: Behavioral objectives provide a good way to correlate learning objectives with test making.)

Behavioral objectives almost always contain the following learning elements:
1. What must be done (an action verb).
2. Under what circumstances and conditions it will take place (the environment).
3. How well it must be done (acceptance level).

Examples of Behavioral Objectives

- Upon examining a state map, the learner will locate and label two navigable rivers in Alabama.
- During a walking tour of the neighborhood adjacent to the school, the learner will classify houses with (1) only deciduous trees, (2) only coniferous trees, (3) both deciduous and coniferous trees, and (4) no trees.
- As a result of polling pupils, the learner will construct and label a bar graph showing how many pupils get to school by (1) walking, (2) school bus, (3) automobile, (4) bicycle, (5) by other means.
- After viewing the filmstrip *Making Graphs*, the learner will demonstrate the construction of a bar graph and a line graph.

Verbs Useful in Writing Social Studies Objectives

cast	identify	categorize	interpret	classify	judge	contrast
label	debate	list	demonstrate	match	design	name
devise	place	draw	plan	express	rank	evaluate
select	frame	separate	group	sort		

Evaluation Form For Methods Class Presentations

Person Presenting Lesson   _____

- Planning   _____

- Interest and Motivation   _____

- Content   _____

- Activity Oriented and Opportunities
  for Pupil Participation   _____

- Time Management   _____

- Poise   _____

- Eye Contact   _____

- Made Clear Explanations   _____

- Checked for Understanding   _____

- Questioning Techniques   _____

- Used Appropriate Materials   _____

- Strategies & Methods   _____

- Knowledge of Subject   _____

- Language Usage   _____

- Teaching Personality   _____

GRADE   _____

EIGHT VITAL TOPICS IN SOCIAL STUDIES TODAY

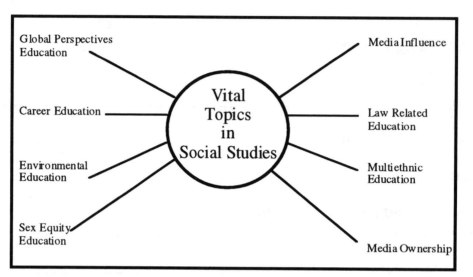

1. **GLOBAL PERSPECTIVES**
    Concepts: Cross-cultural, Transnational, Global System, Conflict, Communication, Interdependence, Third World Nations, Developing Nations, Developed Nations.

2. **ENERGY AND ENVIRONMENTAL EDUCATION**
    Concepts: Environment, Ecosystem, Balance of Nature, Population, Adaptation, Resources, Energy, Pollution, Industrialization.

3. **CAREER EDUCATION -- THE WORLD OF WORK**
    Concepts: Career, Career Families, Work, Leisure, Lifestyle, Occupation, Interests, Values.

4. **LAW-RELATED EDUCATION**
    Concepts: Rules, Laws, Due Process, Authority, Power, Rights, Justice, Privacy, Property, Responsibility, Equal Protection, Legal System.

5. **MULTI-ETHNIC EDUCATION**
    Concepts: Culture, Ethnicity, Ethnocentrism, Pluralism, Heritage, Race, Stereotype, Assimilation, Status, Discrimination, Prejudice, Social Protest.

6. **SEX EQUITY**
    Concepts: Equity, Sex Roles, Sexist Language, Reform Movements, Equality of Opportunity, Nontraditional Roles.

7. **INFLUENCE OF THE MEDIA**
    Concepts: News, Fact, Opinion, Information, Influence, Editor, Radio, Television, Print Media.

8. **WHO OWNS THE MEDIA**
    Concepts: Power, Motive, Ownership, Influence, Obligation.

GROUPING STRATEGIES IN SOCIAL STUDIES

Small-group activity plays a major role in social studies teaching. Group interaction provides pupils with opportunities to work cooperatively in unique ways as they pursue a variety of data-gathering and processing skills.

Common Needs. If a teacher knows that four youngsters need more work with a fundamental map skill, he or she may group those children for aggresive reteaching. The teacher works with them initially to review basic understandings, then the group goes to work independently on a map project that requires application of the understandings.

Common Interests. The class may start a unit by deciding on subtopics to be investigated in the unit, such as religions of the Middle East, festivals of Cajun Louisiana, towns and cities along North American rivers, depletion of rainforest areas, and the like. Children then decide which group they will join by writing first and second choices on a slip of paper. Groups are organized based on topics of expressed interest.

Diverse Talents. Sometimes group tasks have art, writing, or musical components. Each group will need a participant who is talented in one of the components. The teacher identifies specific roles required within each group and children volunteer to fill those roles. An advantage of this is that children begin to see themselves in terms of their unique talents. For example, children who can locate the right reference in the library view themselves as good researchers. Children who can design bulletin boards begin to think of themselves as potential artists.

Social Preference. At times, experienced teachers let students express their choices of co-workers. Each youngster writes the names of two or three others with whom he or she would like to work on a slip of paper. Using this information, the teacher organizes groups so that each child works with at least one chosen person.

Sociograms can be used to gain insight into the social structure of the class. Children are given a hypothetical situation where they must select someone from the class to accompany them on a mission, for example, representing the class in a visit to a hospitalized classmate. Children write choices secretly on a slip of paper and give them to the teacher. By placing the names of all children on a large sheet of paper, the teacher draws arrows (from the chooser to the chosen) to plot the choices. The resulting sociogram allows the teacher to identify children who are chosen infrequently or not at all (called isolates) and find ways to involve them.

USING THE MODALITIES OF LEARNING

The modalities of learning are the ways, methods and manners in which children learn. They are the methods whereby the external bits of information that children receive during periods of learning become internalized.

Visual Mode

The visual mode enables children to learn by what they see. Children today tend to be very visual, due in part to the impact of early exposure to television and other audiovisual technology. School learning can be highly visual in nature. The bulletin board, the chalkboard, filmstrips, movies, computer programs, visual aids such as charts and fingerplays, textbooks, and selective paper-pencil lessons all depend heavily on the child's visual mode.

Auditory Mode

The auditory mode enables children to learn through the sense of hearing. It is very important for young children to listen in order to learn effectively. Primary teachers must verbalize a large amount of information during the average school day. The adjustment-to-school stage alone entails a great deal of telling children what to do. Procedures, organizational skills, acceptable school behavior, and many beginning behaviors are verbalized by teachers.

Tactile Mode

The tactile mode is in operation when children touch, feel, manipulate, order, and use their fine-motor skills. For example, pupils operate within the tactile mode when the class is learning about cities in a mapping lesson. The teacher makes available a large variety of manipulative materials such as building blocks, Lincoln logs, twigs, various kinds of paper, cardboard, yarn, empty containers, boxes, and paints. The children use these materials to construct the buildings, trees, streets, hills, mailboxes, playgrounds, and other physical features of their city on a map layout.

It is important to note that dynamic learning occurs when these three modalities are employed simultaneously. The social studies curriculum in the elementary school is particularly well suited to utilize all three of these modalities: the visual (reading printed materials; viewing movies and filmstrips; examining photos, maps, and charts), the auditory (listening to each other, lectures, cassettes, records), and the tactile (building, sorting, ordering, experiencing texture).

QUESTIONING STRATEGIES

- **Divergent questions** point students in many directions in search of various possible answers. They are most effectively used in the earlier stages of a lesson when students are developing interest in a topic and are seeking information. Divergent questions are generally open ended, allowing many possible responses with no definite right or wrong answers. Example: *Name some ways that we use transportation to get our food.*

- **Convergent questions** focus on one answer and tend to be "remembering" types of questions. For instance, students are called on to remember specific information and responses are verifiable as right or wrong. Convergent questions are designed to converge on the correct answer. Example: *What is the capital of Texas?*

- **Formative questions** are those that provide feedback to the teacher regarding the progress of the lesson, or more specifically, the students' comprehension and application of the lesson objectives. Formative questions are asked during the instructional phase and are ongoing. The specific responses the teacher is given indicate the need for lesson modifications and/or adjustments of various kinds.

- **Summative questions** are those used for evaluative purposes. A summative question is cumulative, concise, and is part of the closure procedure. It is convergent in that the teacher is seeking a response that is a result of the learning that has occurred. Therefore, a summative question is most effective at the end of a lesson. Intermittent quiz questions would be formative (evaluating as learning is occurring) and chapter or unit test questions would be summative (evaluating after learning has occurred). The timing for these questions is the key issue, not necessarily the structural form.

- **Wait Time** (or Think Time) is important. When questions are asked, it is important to allow sufficient think time. Ask the question, then give students time to think about the question and the response. How much think time is enough? Each student or group of students has particular requirements. Experiment to determine the needs of a particular group. Resist the tendency to demand (and accept) an immediate response. Try counting to ten silently before calling on someone.

USING BENJAMIN BLOOM'S TAXONOMY

As teachers, we ask many questions to find out what a learner knows and to encourage thinking. Benjamin Bloom's *Taxonomy of Educational Objectives* provides us with a convenient framework for developing a solid questioning strategy. Questions at the lower level require answers based on knowledge, whereas those at the higher levels require the application of knowledge.

Level One - Knowledge

The Level of Simple Recall: Questions ask for factual information, and answers are either right or wrong.

Example: Name the first president of the United States.

Level Two - Comprehension

The Level of Understanding: Questions ask for reasons. Answers are usually right or wrong.

Example: What do you think the president does?

Level Three - Application

The Level of Usage: Questions usually ask for ways to use knowledge and allow for individual creativity. There may be more than one correct answer.

Example: How can we select a class president?

Level Four - Analysis

The Level of Relationships and Intent: Questions ask for comparisons or for component parts of an idea. Answers are more divergent and personal.

Example: How does the role of the Canadian Prime Minister compare to that of the president of the United States?

Level Five - Synthesis

The Level of Ideas: Questions ask students for ideas for new or different solutions to problems. Answers are creative and divergent; there is no one correct answer.

Example: How would you change the presidency?

Level Six - Evaluation

The Level of Judgment: Questions ask students to make value judgments about ideas of their own or those of others. Answers are very personal, divergent, and sometimes argumentative.

Example: Who is your favorite president and why?

KEY WORDS IN QUESTIONING

A number of key words can be identified in teachers' questions that give students clues to the cognitive level expected in the reply.

1. **Knowledge-Level Questions** (*Remembering*):

define	list	show
describe	name	state
distinguish	recall	tell
identify	recognize	write

2. **Comprehension-Level Questions** (*Understanding*):

compare	estimate	predict
conclude	explain	relate
contrast	extend	rephrase
demonstrate	illustrate	tell in your own words
differentiate	infer	explain the meaning of
distinguish	interpret	give an example of

3. **Application Questions** (*Solving*):

apply	develop	solve
demonstrate	plan	

4. **Analytical Questions** (*Analyzing*):

analyze	compare	distinguish
categorize	contrast	recognize
classify	discriminate	

5. **Synthesis Questions** (*Creating*):

create	formulate	propose
develop	make up	

6. **Evaluation Questions** (*Judging*):

choose	decide	select
evaluate	judge	what do you consider

BIBLIOGRAPHY

BIBLIOGRAPHY

AIDS advocates focus on whether CDC dollars make sense. (1993). *Nation's Health, 23,* (5), 1.

Allen, H., Splittgerber, F., & Manning, M. (1993). *Teaching and learning in the middle level school.* New York: Merrill.

Ammon, R. & Weigard, J. (1993). A look at other trade book topics and genres. In M. Tunnell & R. Ammon (Eds.), *The story of ourselves.* Portsmouth, NH: Heinemann.

Banks, C. & La Grone, S. (1994). The Carter G. Woodson book awards. *Social Education, 58* (5), 316-320.

Banks, J. (1992). Multicultural education: For freedom's sake. *Educational Leadership, 49* (4), 32-35.

Banks, J. (1991). *Teaching strategies for ethnic studies.* (5th ed.) Boston: Allyn and Bacon.

Barr, I. & McGuire, M. (1993). Social studies and effective stories. *Social Studies and the Young Learner, 5* (3), 6-8, 11.

Bean, J. (1992). Creating an integrative curriculum: Making the connections. *NASSP Bulletin, 16* (11), 46-54.

Beck, I. & McKeown, M. (1991). Research directions: Social studies texts are hard to understand: Mediating some of the difficulties. *Language Arts, 68,* 482-489.

Bereiter, C. & Scardamalia, M. (1987). An attainable version of high literacy: Approaches to teaching higher-order skills in reading and writing. *Curriculum Inquiry, 17* (1), 9-30.

Berg, M. (1988). Integrating ideas for social studies. *Social Studies and the Young Learner, 1* (2), pull-out feature.

Boehm, R. & Petersen, J. (1994). An elaboration of the fundamental themes in geography. *Social Education, 58* (4), 211-218.

Bradley Commission on History in Schools. (1988). *Building a history curriculum: Guidelines for teaching history in schools.* Washington, DC: Educational Excellence Network.

California Department of Education. (1987). *California history/social science framework for California public schools, kindergarten through grade twelve.* Sacramento.

Ceprano, M. & English, E. (1990). Fact and fiction: Personalizing social studies through the tradebook-textbook connection. *Reading Horizons, 30,* 66-77.

Chall, J. & Squire, J. (1991). The publishing industry and textbooks. In *The handbook of reading research*, Vol. II, Rebecca Barr, Michael L. Kamil, Peter Mosenthal, and P. David Pearson, eds. New York: Longman.

Chatton, B. (1989). Using literature across the curriculum. In J. Hickman & B. E. Cullinan (Eds.), *Children's literature in the classroom: Weaving Charlotte's web* (pp. 61-70). Needham Heights, MA: Christopher-Gordon.

Cheek, E. & Cheek, M. (1983). *Reading instruction through content teaching.* Columbus, OH: Merrill Publishing Company.

Cooper, H. (1979). Pygmalion grows up: A model for teacher expectation communication and performance influence. *Review of Educational Research, 49*, 389-410.

Craig, A., Graham, W., Kagan, D., Ozment, S., & Turner, F. (1986). *The heritage of world civilizations.* New York: Macmillan Publishing Company.

Cullinan, B. (1993). *Fact and fiction across the curriculum.* Newark, NJ: International Reading Association.

Danielson, K. & LaBonty, J. (1994). *Integrating reading and writing through children's literature.* Boston: Allyn and Bacon.

Davidson, L., Selwyn, D., Palmer, M., & Schwartz, B (1994). An arts-based education: A vision for the future of education. In *ASCD Curriculum Handbook.* (pp. 8.5-8.13). Alexandria, VA: Association for Supervision and Curriculum Development.

Dobson, D., Monson, J., & Smith, J. (1992). A case study on integrating history and reading instruction through literature. *Social Education, 56* (7), 370-375.

Dowd, F. (1990). Geography is children's literature, math, science, art and a whole world of activities. *Journal of Geography, 89*, 68-73.

Drake, S. (1993). *Planning integrated curriculum.* Alexandria, VA: Association of Supervision and Curriculum Development.

Farris, P. & Cooper, S. (1994). *Elementary social studies: A whole language approach.* Madison, WI: WCB Brown & Benchmark Publishers.

Fogarty, R. (1991). Ten ways to integrate curriculum. *Educational Leadership, 49* (10), 24-26.

Fredericks, A. (1992). *The integrated curriculum.* Englewood, CA: Teacher Ideas Press.

Gamberg, R., Kwak, W., Hutchings, M., & Altheim, J. (1988). *Learning and loving it: Theme studies in the classroom.* Portsmouth, NH: Heinemann.

Gehrke, N. (1991). Explorations of teachers' development of integrative curriculums. *Journal of Curriculum and Supervision, 6* (2), 107–117.

Haynes, C. (1986). *Religious freedom in America: A teacher's guide.* Silver Spring, MD: Americans United Research Foundation.

Hennings, D., Hennings, G., & Banich, S. (1993). *Today's elementary social studies.* (2nd ed.). Prospect Heights, IL: Waveland Press.

Huck, C., Hepler, S., & Hickman, J. (1993). *Children's literature in the elementary school* (5th ed.). New York: Holt, Rinehart & Winston.

Hughes, M. (1994). Curriculum integration in the primary grades: A framework for excellence. In *ASCD Curriculum Handbook.* (pp. 11.123-11.194). Alexandria, VA: Association for Supervision and Curriculum Development.

Hunt, N. & Marshall, K. (1994). *Exceptional children and youth: An introduction to special education.* Boston: Houghton Mifflin Company.

Indrisano, R. & Paratore, J. (1992). Using literature with readers at risk. In B. Cullinan (Ed.), *Invitation to read: More children's literature in the reading program* (pp. 138-149). Newark, DE: International Reading Association.

Jacobs, H., & Borland, J. (Fall, 1986). The interdisciplinary concept model: Theory and practice. *Gifted Child Quarterly, 30* (4), 159-163.

Jacobs, H. (1989). *The growing need for interdisciplinary curriculum content.* In H. Jacobs (Ed.), Interdisciplinary curriculum: Design and implementation, pp. 1-12, Alexandria, VA: Association for Supervision and Curriculum Development.

Jacobs, H. (1991). On interdisciplinary education: A conversation. *Educational Leadership, 49* (10), 24-26.

Jarolimek, J. & Parker, W. (1993). *Social studies in elementary education.* New York: Macmillan Publishing Company.

Johnson, N. & Ebert, M. (1992). Time travel is possible: Historical fiction and biography – Passport to the past. *Reading Journal, 45,* 488-495.

Joint Committee on Geographic Education. (1984). *Guidelines for geographic education.* Washington, DC: Association of American Geographers.

Jones, D. (1991). Fourth graders use historical documents and learn citizenship and global awareness. *The Social Studies, 82,* 136-138.

King, E. (1992). Using museums for more effective teaching of ethnic relations. *Journal of Teaching Sociology, 20,* 114-119.

Kuhrt, B. & Farris, P. (1994). Facilitating learning: Strategic instruction in social studies. In Farris, P. & Cooper, S. (Eds.), *Elementary social studies: A whole language approach.* (pp. 131-156). Madison, WI: WCB Brown & Benchmark Publishers.

Ladson-Billings, G. (1994). What we can learn from multicultural education research. *Educational Leadership, 51* (8), 22-26.

Lampe, P. (1988). The problematic nature of interracial and interethnic communication. *The Social Studies, 79,* 116-120.

Lipson, M., Valencia, S., Wixson, K., & Peters, C. (1993). Integration and thematic teaching: Integration to improve teaching and learning. *Language Arts, 70* (4), 252-263.

Louie, B. (1993). Using literature to teach location. *Social Studies and the Young Learner, 5,* 17-18, 22.

Mann, L. (1994). Language arts summary. In *ASCD Curriculum Handbook.* (p. 3.i). Alexandria, VA: Association for Supervision and Curriculum Development.

Martinello, M. & Cook, G. (1994). *Interdisciplinary inquiry in teaching and learning.* New York: Merrill.

Martorella, P. (1994). *Social studies for elementary school children: Developing young citizens.* New York: Merrill.

Maxim, G. (1995). *Social studies and the elementary school child.* (5th ed.) Englewood Cliffs, NJ: Merrill.

Meinbach, A., Rothlein, L, & Fredericks, A. (1995). *The complete guide to thematic units: Creating the integrated curriculum.* Norwood, MA: Christopher-Gordon Publishers.

Michaelis, J. (1992). *Social studies for children: A guide to basic instruction.* Boston: Allyn and Bacon.

Moir, H. (Ed.). (1992). *Collected perspectives: Choosing and using books for the classroom.* Boston: Christopher-Gordon Publishers.

Montagu, A. (1974). *Man's most dangerous myth: The fallacy of race.* (5th ed.) New York: Oxford University Press.

Moss, J. (1984). *Focus in units in literature: A handbook for elementary school teachers.* Urbana, IL: National Council of Teachers of English.

National Council of Teachers of Mathematics. (1989). *Curriculum and evaluation standards for school mathematics.* Reston, VA: National Council of Teachers of Mathematics.

Norris, D. (1991). Global interdependence: Learning from personal effects. *Social Education, 55* (6), 371-373.

O'Brien, B. & Walter, J. (1994). Visual and performing arts principles: Content and organization. In *ASCD Curriculum Handbook.* (pp. 8.37-8.39). Alexandria, VA: Association for Supervision and Curriculum Development.

Piaget, J. (1952). *The origins of intelligence in children.* New York: International Universities Press.

Pugh, S., & Garcia, J. (1992). Multicultural trade books for adolescents: A definition and sampler. *Social Education, 56* (5), 303-306.

Religion in the curriculum. (1987). Alexandria, VA: Association for Supervision and Curriculum Development.

Robinson, F. (1970). *Effective Study,* 4th ed. New York: Harper & Row.

Routman, R. (1991). *Invitations: Changing as teachers and learners K-12.* Portsmouth, NH: Heinemann.

Rubenstein, J. (1989). *The cultural landscape: An introduction to human geography.* (2nd ed.). Columbus, OH: Merrill Publishing.

Rubin, D. (1993). *A practical approach to teaching reading.* 2nd Edition. Boston: Allyn and Bacon.

Samuels, S. (1988). Decoding and automaticity: Helping poor readers become automatic at word recognition. *The Reading Teacher, 41,* 756-760.

Sesow, F., Van Cleaf, D., & Chadwick, B. (1992). Investigating classroom cultures. *Social Studies and the Young Learner, 4* (3), 3-5.

Sherman, H. (1993). An international store to integrate global awareness, math, and social studies. *Social Studies and the Young Learner, 6* (1), 17-18.

Skeel, D. (1995). *Elementary social studies: Challenges for tomorrow's world.* New York: Harcourt Brace College Publishers.

Smith, C. (1994). Integrated language arts. In *ASCD Curriculum Handbook.* (pp. 3.22-3.23). Alexandria, VA: Association for Supervision and Curriculum Development.

Stafford, J. (1993). How to teach about religions in the elementary social studies classroom. *The Social Studies, 84,* 245-248.

Stewig, J. (1992). Using children's books as a bridge to other cultures. *The Social Studies, 53* (1), 36-40.

Stockard, J., & Wolfinger, D. (in press). *Social studies for the elementary school child: An interdisciplinary approach.* Needham Heights, MA: Allyn & Bacon.

Stopsky, F. & Lee, S. (1994). *Social Studies in a Global Society.* Albany, NY: Delmar Publishers, Inc.

Sunal, C. (1990). *Early childhood social studies.* Columbus, OH: Merrill Publishing Company.

Taba, H. (1962). *Curriculum development: Theory and practice.* New York: Harcourt Brace Jovanovich.

Tomasino, K. (1993). Literature and social studies: A spicy mix for fifth graders. *Social Studies and the Young Learner, 5* (4), 7-10.

Tye, K. (Ed.). (1990). *Global education: From thought to action.* Yearbook of the Association for Supervision and Curriculum Development. Alexandria, VA.

Winfield, L. (1989). Teacher beliefs toward at-risk students in inner-urban schools. *The Urban Review, 18,* 253-267.

Wright, J. (1966). *Human nature in geography.* Cambridge, MA: Harvard University Press.

Zarnowski, M. (1990). *Learning with biographies: A reading and writing approach.* Washington, DC: National Council for the Social Studies and National Council of Teachers of English

ABOUT THE AUTHOR

Dr. James W. Stockard, Jr. is Associate Professor of Elementary Education in the Department of Early Childhood, Elementary, and Reading Education at Auburn University at Montgomery. He teaches undergraduate methods courses and graduate curriculum courses in elementary school social studies. Dr. Stockard served for twenty-seven years in the Caddo Parish School System (Shreveport, Louisiana) as a sixth-grade teacher, supervisor of elementary education, director of middle schools, and assistant superintendent in charge of curriculum and instruction. Dr. Stockard serves as the Executive Secretary of the Alabama Council for the Social Studies, and he formerly served on the Board of Directors and as Vice President of the Southeast Regional Social Studies Conference. He has written two new textbooks which are due for publication in 1996: *Social Studies for the Elementary School Child: An Interdisciplinary Approach*, published by Allyn and Bacon, and *Elementary Methods: An Integrated Curriculum*, published by Longman.